Daring, Thrilling, Baffling

HARRY HOUDINI

Fifty years after his last performance, Houdini is still the world's most famous mystifier. Now, for the first time in paperback, the secrets of the incredible exploits that enthralled the world . . .

Details of spectacular stage illusions:

Walking Through a Brick Wall,
The Spanish Maiden Escape,
The Milk Can Challenge

Plus many more such marvelous feats

· Rope ties · chain releases · underwater escapes
· Box, trunk, barrel and coffin escapes

THE GREAT SECRETS OF THE SHOWMAN WHO MYSTIFIED THE WORLD

Bantam Books by Walter B. Gibson

HOUDINI'S ESCAPES
HOUDINI'S MAGIC

ABOUT THE AUTHOR

WALTER B. GIBSON, after completing *Houdini's Escapes* and *Houdini's Magic*, turned to fiction writing, creating the famed mystery character of Lamont Cranston, also known as the Shadow. Under the pen name of Maxwell Grant, he wrote novel-length stories for *The Shadow Magazine* for more than fifteen years. These novels were adapted for the Shadow radio program and today they are being reprinted in paperback and hardcover editions. Under his own name, Mr. Gibson has written *The Master Magicians* and many other books in the fields of magic, games and the occult.

HOUDINI'S ESCAPES

PREPARED FROM HOUDINI'S PRIVATE NOTEBOOKS AND
MEMORANDA WITH THE ASSISTANCE OF BEATRICE HOUDINI,
WIDOW OF HOUDINI, AND BERNARD M. L. ERNST,
PRESIDENT OF THE PARENT ASSEMBLY OF THE SOCIETY
OF AMERICAN MAGICIANS

by WALTER B. GIBSON

Introduction by
Milbourne Christopher

BANTAM BOOKS
TORONTO · NEW YORK · LONDON

HOUDINI'S ESCAPES

*A Bantam Book/published by arrangement with
Funk & Wagnalls Publishing Company, Inc.*

PRINTING HISTORY
*Originally published by Blue Ribbon Books,
Harcourt Brace in 1930*

Funk & Wagnalls edition (part of a two volume book,
HOUDINI'S ESCAPES AND MAGIC) *published January 1976*

Bantam edition/November 1976

Photographs of Houdini courtesy of Culver Pictures, Inc.

*Bantam Books are published by Bantam Books, Inc. Its trade-
mark, consisting of the words "Bantam Books" and the por-
trayal of a bantam, is registered in the United States Patent
Office and in other countries. Marca Registrada. Bantam
Books, Inc., 666 Fifth Avenue, New York, New York 10019.*

PRINTED IN THE UNITED STATES OF AMERICA

0 9 8 7 6 5 4 3 2 1

INTRODUCTION

by Milbourne Christopher

A new generation, caught up in the biggest magic boom since the heyday of vaudeville, is enthralled by the incredible exploits of Houdini. Books, films, television and radio documentaries, and magazine and newspaper features have presented thrilling, if frequently fanciful, accounts of his feats. This dynamic showman, a critic noted, could get out of manacles quicker than most people get out of bed. No restraining device could hold him; Houdini released himself from welded cylinders, government jails, and submerged iron-banded boxes—without leaving a clue to his methods.

How did "the Elusive American" do it? Sir Arthur Conan Doyle thought he knew. The creator of Sherlock Holmes stated unequivocally that his friend was a powerful medium. How else could he free himself, wrists shackled four feet apart in a position that made it impossible for him to reach a duplicate key, or a lock pick? Conan Doyle also insisted there was no "normal way" for Houdini to penetrate a paper bag or a "sealed glass tank" without ripping the first or smashing the second.

Earlier, J. Hewat MacKenzie, president of the British College of Psychic Science, had been on a London stage when Houdini was locked in an airtight, water-filled container, then enclosed in a curtained cabinet. Moments before the drenched escapologist burst through the drapes, MacKenzie felt a draft. This, he stated, was positive proof that Houdini had dematerialized his body and oozed out.

An explanation for Houdini's escape from a challenge packing crate was advanced by a woman who saw him during a record-breaking nine-month run at Keith's

Theatre in Boston. She said Mrs. Houdini, concealed in the cabinet that covered the box, freed him by extracting the nails with a magnet. Another spectator disagreed. In her opinion, the man who came forward to accept the applause was a double. Houdini, she continued, stayed in the crate until his assistants released him after the show.

So much for conjectures. Practical instructions for the box-escapes and the feats Conan Doyle and MacKenzie said were done with psychic aid are to be found in the pages that follow.

Houdini died at the age of fifty-two in Detroit on October 31, 1926. Later, his widow and his lawyer sent stacks of the notes he had made through the years to his friend, Walter B. Gibson. Houdini had written three manuals—*Handcuff Secrets, Magical Rope Ties and Escapes*, and *Paper Magic*; he had hoped to produce more.

It was not an easy task for Gibson, a facile writer and a clever conjurer, to prepare this material for publication. Houdini jotted down not only his own methods, but those of his rivals. Some descriptions were brief and required amplification, others were more extensive and sometimes repetitive. Occasionally a sketch would explain more than pages of text. It is fortunate this work is in print. Some of Houdini's notes, all of which Gibson returned, have since disappeared.

It will soon become apparent to the reader that, though Houdini was daring, he never took an uncalculated risk. He would not accept a challenge unless he was sure he could meet it. He was physically fit, an athlete, and a strong swimmer. Yet his assistants were poised to rescue him if he didn't surface on schedule from an underwater box. A dozen less careful performers have been drowned, or seriously injured, because they attempted this feat without sufficient knowledge, or without taking precautions.

Houdini experimented constantly, striving to make his escapes and his magic more effective. This sustained effort, plus his marvelous showmanship, enabled him to become a legend during his lifetime. Fifty years after his last performance, Houdini still is the world's most famous mystifier.

Contents

Part Three. SPECIAL CHALLENGES

Part Four. BOX ESCAPES

Part Five. UNDER-WATER ESCAPES

Part Six. TRUNKS—BARRELS—COFFINS

Part Seven. MISCELLANEOUS ESCAPES

Part Eight. SPECTACULAR MYSTERIES
AND ESCAPES

PREFACE

by Bernard M. L. Ernst

Had Houdini lived he would have written this book. He planned to write a number of books other than those which were published during his lifetime. Among them was to be the first-hand story of his unusual and remarkable career and accomplishments. A volume on the lives of famous magicians was to follow. A work on plagiarism was contemplated and an authoritative exposure of the methods and devices of fraudulent mediums. A number of books on controversial subjects were also planned as well as a series of essays and treatises on magic and finally an encyclopedia of magic and kindred art.

He had gathered a mass of material for all of these contemplated publications and in some cases had prepared parts of his manuscript. In *M.U.M.*, the official journal of the Society of American Magicians of which he was the president, and elsewhere, he had published serially much of his material dealing with the lives of famous magicians; and he also had dictated many chapters of his autobiography. These, unfortunately, were lost during his life, to his great regret and discomfiture.

During the summer of 1926, only a few months before his death, he sent me a mass of material including rough notes, drawings, blue prints, and manuscripts, with the request that it be arranged, edited and published in a series of books on magic and escapes with which his name should be connected. Much of the material in this book is taken from this source.

More than a year before, while staying with Mrs. Houdini at my home at Sea Cliff, L.I., he had begged me to examine a trunkful of his material and write one or more of the books which he was eager to publish and which he never found time to write himself. He described what he had gathered together and insisted that many of his ideas and inventions had never been thought of or made public. As late as October 9, 1926, the last day he was in New York, before his death at Detroit, Mich., on October 31, 1926, he again spoke to me at my home about the projected books, and referred to additional material he had for such use. After his death, Mrs. Beatrice Houdini, his widow, knowing of his plans and familiar with his collections, sent this additional material, a part of which also appears in Mr. Gibson's work. Indeed during Houdini's life Mr. Gibson had practically completed two volumes of a proposed series of books on "small magic" along lines projected by Houdini; but because of the latter's untimely death the publication of these works was abandoned.

Houdini made it plain that certain of his greatest and most distinctive escapes were never to be made public. Among these was his escape from the so-called Chinese Water Torture Cell, which he used in vaudeville for many years and which he referred to as his "upside down." Other methods and escapes now used by professional magicians are also withheld from publication in justice and fairness to conjurers generally. The contents of this book have been referred to the Committee on Exposures of the Society of American Magicians and to Hardeen, Houdini's brother, who is using many of Houdini's effects upon the stage, and deletions have been made as suggested by them. Magic exposed is deprived of mystery and ceases to be magic—at least for entertainment purposes and use in the theater. Thus the vanishing of an elephant from a cabinet on a full lighted stage as done by Houdini and many similar illusions of the professional performer are omitted here.

Many releases from restraints, however, at one time or another used by Houdini or devised by him, are published, it is believed, for the first time, and many of the creations of his ingenious mind now find their way into print as he intended. The reader will be amazed at the simplicity in some cases and at the complexity in others of the devices and methods employed or originated by the master of escapes, the "handcuff king," the man whose power of releasing himself has been described by Sir Arthur Conan Doyle and others as being supernormal and super-natural. In his book entitled *Spirit Intercourse*, J. Hewat McKenzie, president of the British College of Psychic Science, writes: "The force necessary to shoot a bolt within a lock is drawn from Houdini, the medium, but it must not be thought that this is the only means by which he can escape from his prison, for at times his body has been dematerialized and withdrawn." Houdini's reply was in part as follows: "I do not claim to free myself from the restraint of fetters and confinement, but positively state that I accomplish my purpose purely by physical, not psychical, means. My methods are perfectly natural, resting on natural laws of physics. I do not *dematerialize* or *materialize* anything: I simply control and manipulate material things in a manner perfectly well understood by myself, and thoroughly accountable for and equally understandable (if not duplicable) by any person to whom I may elect to divulge my secrets."

Some of the secrets of Houdini as communicated to me and as put in the writings which he gave to me are found in the pages which follow. Many of his effects were so hazardous and nerve-racking that no one, even if familiar with the *modus operandi*, would have the courage, physical ability, or temerity to attempt to duplicate them.

There has been only one Houdini and he is gone.

Part One

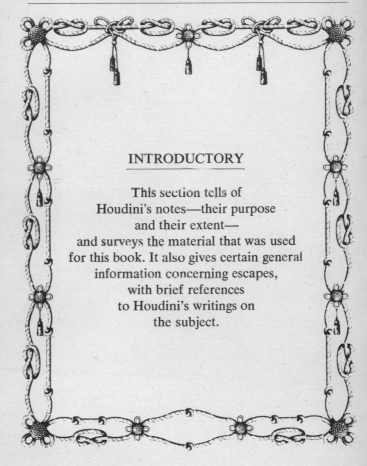

INTRODUCTORY

This section tells of
Houdini's notes—their purpose
and their extent—
and surveys the material that was used
for this book. It also gives certain general
information concerning escapes,
with brief references
to Houdini's writings on
the subject.

HOUDINI'S NOTES

The notes left by Houdini form a remarkable collection of material on methods of escape, magical tricks and illusions, and spiritualistic effects. Of these, the methods of escape constitute a large and interesting portion. Houdini was famous as a magician and as an exposer of fraudulent spiritualistic phenomena, but it is an undeniable fact that he gained his great reputation through his sensational escape tricks, which he performed during the early years of the present century. Millions of people remember Houdini as the man who "could get out of anything," and public interest finds a natural center in this particular branch of his work.

The notes which Houdini left are of great variety. Some of his most important escapes are not covered by them. The reason is that these notes were intended primarily for his own reference. Methods that were already built or in operation did not require written descriptions; in fact, Houdini made it a practice not to set them down in writing. The system he employed—so far as his note-making had a system— was to put down any idea that occurred to him as suitable for an escape. In some of these notations he offered no solution whatever; in others, he gave a rough idea of how the escape might be accomplished. Some ended at this point; on other escapes, he made additional notes, or new notes which gave more definite ideas of working methods. Occasionally he mentioned when and where he had employed the escape in the manner described; with others, there is no definite evidence that he actually used the escape or that it proved entirely practicable as explained.

The best of Houdini's notes were found in a looseleaf book. Records of the methods were typewritten and illustrated with pen or pencil sketches. Other notes were typewritten on separate sheets of paper, some

written in ink in longhand, and others penciled on
steamship and hotel paper. Houdini was an active
enthusiast; whenever he heard of or saw a new form of
restraint, his mind began to work on it, and he made his
notes accordingly. Some of his notes are ideas; others
are plans; others are finished effects. All of them, in the
final analysis, are Houdini's methods. In the present
volume, the plan has been to adhere as closely as possible to the notes themselves, supplying certain statements that are obviously to be understood, and endeavoring to make plain Houdini's methods from the
information that he himself supplied. Elaborate working diagrams are not included, for they did not appear
in the explanations, which should not be misrepre-
sented. The "revelations" that have been made by certain writers who have advanced questionable claims to
knowledge of Houdini's secrets are notoriously inac-
curate and are not in accord with his actual notes.

It should be remembered that there is a vast difference between the description of a trick or an escape and
its actual presentation. Properly exhibited on the stage,
a very simple device becomes a seeming miracle. The
artfulness of any deception lies in introducing simplicity
where people look for complexity, and this is evident in
many of Houdini's methods. Some of the escapes included in the notes are the outgrowth of suggestions
given to Houdini; others are improvements or additions
to older methods. These are presented in this book.

There are definite indications that Houdini intended
to publish his notes, or a considerable portion of them.
One trick carries, instead of an explanation, the statement that he did not wish the secret to become known.
A few of the tricks were typed ready for publication,
but there is very little evidence of any definite arrangement. The chief difficulty encountered in the legible
notes consists in references to other methods that are
missing from the records, or that were never set down.
When two escapes depended upon a similar mechanical
device, Houdini has said that the one works like the

other; but without a description of the first escape, the second is incomplete.

Had Houdini undertaken the writing of a book from this available material, he would necessarily have prepared preliminary chapters dealing with escape methods, following these with the secrets in the notes, clearing up obscure points, and adding further material from memory. Remarks of a preliminary nature were lacking, but this material has been supplied as a résumé of Houdini's little books on *Handcuff Secrets* and *Rope Ties and Escapes* and from other sources. The actual notes cover all types of escapes and give an excellent insight into working methods employed by Houdini. Further material that he may have intended to publish cannot, of course, be supplied.

Only those escapes of which some explanation is given are included. Some of them are not in the final state of development that Houdini would have demanded prior to presenting them in public. But in each instance, the fundamental principle of operation is described; and it was upon such fundamental principles that Houdini based all his finished escapes.

HOUDINI'S METHODS

Despite the fact that a prominent spiritualist once declared that Houdini was a medium who made his escapes by dematerializing himself and then resuming his material form, the average person is aware that Houdini was a normal individual who accomplished his escapes by physical methods. There are, however, two popular misconceptions regarding Houdini: one that he was a veritable contortionist who could slip his hands through the tightest handcuffs and accomplish acts that seemed physically impossible; the other that he relied entirely upon mysterious, phenomenal secrets that were almost beyond human understanding, and that these secrets died with him. As a matter of fact, Houdini did possess great physical strength and agility that enabled him to accomplish escapes impossible or too difficult for the great majority of people. He also had secret methods which he kept to himself and of which he left no trace. But both of these were merely adjuncts to his work.

The greatest factor in Houdini's success was his showmanship. He knew how to present his escapes so that they were both amazing and spectacular; and with his ability as a showman he also possessed a thorough knowledge of every form or type of escape. He was familiar with every type of lock and every make of handcuff. He was constantly experimenting and inventing new tools and appliances. His natural ingenuity and his long experience gave him full confidence in his ability to meet any challenge or to attempt any form of escape. Houdini could employ a regular escape, using a method well known among escape artists, and present it with the same effectiveness that marked the other items of his program. On the contrary, there were escapes in Houdini's repertoire that could not have been successfully accomplished by his imitators even if he had given them the instructions.

Furthermore, if both Houdini and another performer had presented a similar escape under similar conditions, the average audience would have received Houdini's work with much more enthusiasm and wonderment than that accorded the other performer. This was because Houdini had the personality and the showmanship to exhibit a type of performance that offered numerous obstacles to effective presentation. Consider one of Houdini's challenge performances from the standpoint of a spectator. Attracted to the theater by large advertisements, the spectator watched a committee bind Houdini or secure him in some form of restraint. Then, while the orchestra played, the audience waited during a period that might vary from ten minutes to an hour, while Houdini was out of sight in his cabinet. At the conclusion of this period, Houdini made his appearance, free.

The spectator came to see Houdini make a sensational escape; he saw him bound; he saw him free; he did not see the actual escape. Yet he was highly pleased with the performance! Why? Because Houdini was a showman to the nth power. His greatest secret was his own showmanship. He possessed the ability to rouse the interest of his audiences to such a pitch that it would not decrease while he was out of sight. No one left the theater during his prolonged escapes. People were held there by an irresistible desire to await Houdini's accomplishment of his task.

To Houdini belongs the credit of bringing the escape act into popularity and using it to build up a lasting fame. There was only one Houdini, and there will never be another. He was a genius who could apply all his effort to practical purposes, and who relied on research and hard work as much as on inspiration. There were other performers who sought fame as escape artists, and some of them used methods in certain escapes that were similar to those employed by Houdini. But their knowledge was superficial when compared to his, and most of them made the mistake of imitating his work. The escape act is recognized as a type of magic or mystery that is dependent on certain useful and fundamental principles. Houdini was the originator of many new methods; some became known to the profession; others were copied very closely. Houdini was not radical in his work; it is evident from his notes that he relied on accepted methods, but increased their effectiveness by improving or disguising them. He possessed the three qualities essential to a great mystifier: inventive genius, mechanical ability, and showmanship.

The very difficulty that Houdini so splendidly overcame in the presentation of his work, namely, the holding of interest while he was out of sight of the audience, served him well in the protection of his methods and secrets. When a trick or an illusion is performed in full view, it is seen through all stages of its operation. An escape from a device concealed in a cabinet is not seen during its most important stage. Therefore it may perplex the best-trained observer, who can only attempt to invent a way in which the trick could be done, and trust to luck that he has found the method actually used.

Houdini had a very practical mind. His notes show that in devising escapes he frequently chose the simplest and most direct way to obtain the results he desired, then depended on his showmanship and his ability as a performer to make the escape effective. He constantly made improvements; his ideas were limitless, and he was never satisfied with an escape until he knew that it could be done effectively. The brief summaries of escape work that follow this introduction may therefore be regarded as a partial explanation of Houdini's methods. It may be said that Houdini made use of these principles whenever necessary, but discarded them when he invented newer or better methods. For Houdini was an escape artist extraordinary, a master in his chosen field, and the fact that his work so completely mystified the public stands as a proof of his remarkable capabilities.

THE ESCAPE ACT

Houdini set the standard for the escape act; his work received great popular acclamation, and he surpassed all rivals in that field. His escapes were of various types, and they come under two distinct groups: challenges and straight escapes. In the former, Houdini allowed his challengers to bring their own appliances and lock him in; in the latter, he was confined in specially built apparatus of his own construction, subject to thorough examination by a committee from the audience.

The advantage of challenges lay in the fact that they offered opportunities for advertising and also proved a special attraction that led to capacity audiences. Their disadvantage lay in the fact that they were not routine work, and therefore presented problems that must be solved quickly. There was also the element of uncertainty in a new challenge, and for this reason Houdini preferred challenges that had been used before and that had proven effective and interesting to the audiences that witnessed them.

New challenges sometimes came unexpectedly. The old ones were usually arranged in whatever city Houdini was playing. A local concern supplied a packing box, a brewery supplied a barrel, or other devices were employed. All such challenges were bona fide, the stipulations being that the apparatus should be built a few days in advance, and that certain specifications as to size and construction be followed.

In straight escape work, Houdini used contrivances that were very convincingly built, and gave every one a good opportunity to satisfy himself that the apparatus was strong and secure. With his own escapes, Houdini could present a regular act that would, except in unexpected circumstances, run through on a fairly regular schedule. In handcuff escapes, challenges were accepted; but in dealing with the usual handcuffs, these performances were very close to routine work. In most of his escapes, Houdini used a cabinet, executing the escape out of sight. In others, such as the straitjacket escape, he performed the feat in full view of the audience. This type of work was desirable and practical whenever the escape depended entirely on effort and strenuous exertion. Where mechanical means were employed, the cabinet was usually essential in order to protect the secret.

In escaping from contrivances built by challengers, Houdini required tools with which to work his way out. These are mentioned in his notes; the means of their concealment is not always explained. It was not a difficult matter for him to hide the required tools on his person, especially as very few were required for most of the escapes. Inasmuch as the possession of tools would afford no explanation of the average escape, it was an easy matter for him to avoid a thorough search by committee-men. In some cases, however, bulky implements were required; and in such instances special precautions must have been used to conceal the appliances. Some of the large escapes explained in Houdini's notes were designed to operate without the aid of any appliances; this was a desirable factor.

It is a known fact that Houdini was thoroughly searched on various occasions, and effected his escape from jails and prisons with no apparent means of obtaining any tools or keys to assist him. It is obvious that the more formidable the escape, the less interested is the committee in searching the performer for hidden appliances. Boxes, trunks, and other apparatus locked on the outside seem secure in themselves. In jail-breaking, where instruments seemed specially desirable, an escape would not have been effective without a thorough search. Whenever Houdini escaped from a prison cell, he emphasized the fact that he had no keys or lock-picking devices on his person.

The jail escape may be classed as a challenge. None of Houdini's notes refer to it. Included with the notes was a pamphlet published in England that covers the subject of jail-breaking but does not satisfactorily explain the majority of Houdini's spectacular escapes of this type. The presence of this pamphlet with the notes indicates that Houdini might have included prison escapes in the contemplated book; the absence of notes on the subject does not point to the contrary, as Houdini was so thoroughly familiar with this type of escape work that he could have supplied all necessary information from memory. Most of his celebrated prison escapes were performed early in his career; Houdini did not include them among his future plans, and it is noticeable that in the notebooks he avoided descriptions of secrets which did not have a definite bearing on contemplated escapes.

The methods of imitators who sought to perform the jail escape could not have survived the severe tests to which Houdini submitted. Any one can get out of a prison cell by "fixing" it with the police, and it is a known fact that self-styled "escape kings" have resorted to this practice. Houdini made bona fide escapes from prisons; and the police certificates that he received are permanent proof of that fact. He spared no effort to show the world that his escapes were genuine and that they were made in spite of every possible measure to prevent them.

Houdini sought new challenges, but in his later career he limited his work to those which had proven most effective. Similarly he looked for spectacular effects in his straight escape work and, during his final years, the only escape that he regularly performed was the Chinese Water Torture Cell, which was quick, spectacular, and effective.

HANDCUFF ESCAPES

Houdini explained the methods of escaping from handcuffs in his book entitled *Handcuff Secrets*, and certain of his introductory notes in that volume are of interest.

They are quoted here in part:

"In writing this book on handcuff tricks, and allied mysteries, I simply do so as a great many people imagine you must have exceptionally rare talent to become a handcuff king, but such is not the case. The primary lesson is, to learn to use both hands with equal facility, as—if I may use a proverbial expression—one hand washes the other, but in this case one hand releases the other. The method adopted by me to acquire this end was, when at table I practiced to use the left hand persistently, until I could use it almost as easily as the right.

"You will notice that some of these tricks are very simple—but remember it is not the trick that is to be considered, but the style and manner in which it is presented.

"I do not *deliberately say* that the following methods given are precisely the same as I have used on opening the handcuffs or in performing the various other sundry acts, but I speak with absolute confidence when I assert that these are the methods that can be, and have been, used to imitate my performances without much outlay and with little practice."

The third paragraph quoted supports the assumption that Houdini depended on presentation as much as method. The italics in the third paragraph carry the impression that Houdini actually used the methods he described in the book; and it is highly probable that he used other methods which he did not explain.

Regular handcuffs are made alike; that is, all of one pattern may be unlocked by the standard key. The performer insists that all handcuffs brought upon the stage be of a regulation pattern. He is provided with keys of all makes and is thus enabled to unlock the cuffs when in the cabinet. The locks of all handcuffs are not reachable when the hands are bound; therefore special keys have been designed, fitted with extension rods so that they can be manipulated by the hand. Others may be opened by holding the key in the teeth. Certain forms of regulation handcuffs may be opened without keys. Houdini stated that "you can open the majority of the old-time cuffs with a shoestring. By simply making a loop in the string, you can lasso the end of the screw in the lock and yank the bolt back, and so open the cuff in as clean a manner as if opened with the original key." He also explained that cuffs can be opened by striking them against a plate of lead fastened underneath the trousers at the knee or by striking them upon a block of metal.

The greatest problem in opening regulation cuffs is the concealment of the keys. They may be hidden in a bag strapped around the knee, or somewhere else on the performer's person. They may also be hidden in the cabinet where the performer retires to make his escape; details of the cabinet appear later in this book. Or they may be smuggled to the performer by an assistant, this last method requiring only the keys that are needed for the particular cuffs that have been brought up by the committee.

There are also various forms of trick handcuffs— that is, regular cuffs that have been faked in some ingenious manner. These can stand inspection; when locked on a person who does not know the secret, escape is impossible; but the performer can open such cuffs automatically. The escape artist who uses such handcuffs usually has them brought on the stage by a confederate, who hands them in with others brought by genuine committee-men.

Among various instruction sheets that were with Houdini's notes is an ingenious idea for coping with strange handcuffs of which the performer is doubtful. The performer has keys of all descriptions, and in examining the challenger's handcuffs he or his assistant notes the key that unlocks the challenger's cuffs. This is "switched" for a key that resembles it; the performer thus gains possession of the genuine key and uses it, making another exchange after the escape, while the challenger is looking over the cuffs that the performer has opened.

The performer who attempts handcuff escapes must be familiar with all patterns of cuffs, must be provided with the necessary keys and implements, must hide these instruments effectively, and must be ready for any emergency. There are various artifices whereby difficult or doubtful cuffs may be avoided. A cuff that cannot be opened may be put on the wrists after several other handcuffs have been placed there; being high up on the forearm, it can be slipped over the wrists after the other cuffs are removed. It is readily seen that there are limitations according to the performer's knowledge and ability, and the information given here simply reveals a few of the fundamental methods.

Houdini's knowledge of this subject was tremendous. He studied all types of handcuffs and was so experienced in opening them that he could accept any challenge that was offered. His book on *Handcuff Escapes* contains enough useful information to enable a capable person to become a good escape artist, but it is only a partial exposé of Houdini's total knowledge of this subject.

Opening padlocks with special keys or picks is another phase of escape work that comes under the heading of handcuff escapes, and Houdini also revealed many essential methods of lock-picking. Houdini devised a split master key that was patented in England and that could open the different styles of regular handcuffs used in the British Isles. None of Houdini's imitators possessed more than a fraction of his knowledge of locks; hence they relied upon faked handcuffs and were limited in their work. They used methods similar to those employed by Houdini on certain forms of standard cuffs, but Houdini's knowledge was so much greater that his work really began where others' ended.

ROPE TIES

In his book, *Magical Rope Ties and Escapes*, Houdini reveals the fundamental methods of this type of escape work. Apart from actual tricks with ropes, there are many effective ways of handling ropes so that escapes from them are less difficult. In contrast to handcuffs, which are rigid and are placed on a performer in one single, direct operation, ropes may be placed in many ways and tied with a multitude of knots. It is an old saying that "you can't beat a man at his own game," and this applies directly to rope ties. The man who is experienced in getting out of ropes—and Houdini was the master of this art—invariably "knows the ropes" better than the persons who seek to bind him.

The average person plays easily into the performer's hands. There are various positions in which a man may be tied that look very difficult, yet that are easy for purposes of release. Slack, slip-knots, pliable rope that is easily untied—all these are advantages to the performer. Even sailors, with their knowledge of intricate knots, are not ordinarily accustomed to tying persons; and the skillful performer can usually master any situation they create. Houdini could untie the most intricate knots with his hands, ordinary knots with his teeth, and some knots with his feet. He was always ready to accept any challenge in which ropes were involved, but there were occasions on which he encountered unexpected difficulties. Here he depended largely on his strength and endurance. He evidently worked on the theory that the release from any arrangement of ropes was merely a matter of time, and he always kept on until he was free.

Rope ties depend considerably on the limitations of the performer. The man of slight physical strength and small skill in untying knots can escape from some rope ties, but he must depend on favorable positions and certain types of knots. These factors were useful to Houdini also, and he never neglected them; but he was virtually without limitations in this work; his ability was so far above the average that he could attempt escapes that others would have found impossible. There is one other factor in rope ties that is of tremendous advantage to the escape artist; that is, ropes can be cut. With a knife available—especially when the performer is hidden in a cabinet—there is one way out of virtually every emergency.

A few paragraphs from Houdini's book on *Rope Ties* will prove illuminating. They refer to the Clothes Line Tie, in which the performer is bound with about sixty feet of sash cord.

"The whole secret lies in the fact that it is quite impossible to tie a man while in a standing position, with such a length of rope, so that he cannot squirm out of it with comparative ease, if the tying begins at one end of the rope and finishes at the other. . . .

"It is the experience of all who have used this tie, that the first few knots are carefully tied, but after a time it will be found that the rope is being used up very slowly, and they will begin winding it around the body and making very few knots. . . .

"If the committee . . . begin to make more knots than suits you, it will be well to swell the muscles, expand the chest, slightly hunch the shoulders, and hold the arm a little away from the sides. After a little practice you will find that such artifices will enable you to balk the most knowing ones. You should always wear a coat when submitting to this tie, as that will be found to be an added help in obtaining slack. . . .

"A sharp knife with a hook-shaped blade should be concealed somewhere on the person, as it may be found useful in case some of the first, carefully tied knots, prove troublesome. A short piece cut from the end of the rope will never be missed."

Certain qualities of rope are more readily adapted to escapes than others. Houdini mentions this both in his book on *Rope Ties* and in his notes. In all escapes it is preferable for the performer to supply his own rope; in accepting challenges the type of rope used can usually be specified by him.

Rope is rope, so far as the public is concerned, and it is so easily examined that suspicion is seldom attached to it.

The following statement on rope ties was among Houdini's notes:

"There are many types of rope ties and in all of them the secret of escape depends on the ability of the one being secured to gain the necessary slack for a starter. Just as with the straitjacket, it becomes necessary to gain the first slack. It may be done by 'misguiding' the tier or by main muscular strength of the tied. In either case, once secured, the escape can be effectually made."

HOUDINI'S CABINETS

In the great majority of his escapes, Houdini used a cabinet, and all other escape artists have invariably followed the same custom. The cabinet must not only be unsuspicious in appearance; it must stand an examination by committee members, who go through it before the escape takes place. Houdini's notes on special cabinets are in the form of reference, listing arrangements for a new scene cabinet; hence they do not give complete details; they show that a cabinet can, if desired, be well equipped with special appliances. In many of his regulation escapes, Houdini utilized an ordinary cabinet which was exactly what it appeared to be: a light framework, suitable for easy packing, with curtains hanging from horizontal rods. The more elaborate cabinets were not part of Houdini's regular act; they were ideas that he evidently considered of possible value in certain forms of escape work.

The notes on a *new scene cabinet* include the following:

"First, a small tube, or opening fitted into the side or back of the cabinet; this to allow an assistant to slide in any special key or device which might be required. Such a system would make it unnecessary to stock the cabinet with small appliances; these could be obtained from off-stage and slipped in after the inspection."

The notes mention "places to hide 'gags'; knife, ropes, cuffs, belt, plug 8 'fakes,'[1] files, extensions, etc." The suitable places for concealment were secret pockets or ornamental trimmings of the curtains, or the top of the cabinet. The horizontal bars at the top of the cabinet afforded an excellent hiding-place for keys. These bars are made of tubing; the upper portion, when cut away, is not visible, and the recess serves as a long container where articles are laid in a regular, orderly row. Where ropes were used, Houdini planned an arrangement to bring out a knife in any position, for the cutting of ropes and straps. This is not described in detail; probably it was fitted into one of the corner posts of the cabinet. A chair was sometimes used in the cabinet, the bottom of one leg fitted with a slot into which keys or fakes could be inserted so that the performer could work on handcuffs without using his hands. This chair is described among the notes. The chair also had possibilities as a place for concealing small articles. The cabinet was designed to hide numerous articles up to the size of saws. As its secret was never detected, it is certain that all the places of concealment were ingeniously devised.

Houdini's notes describe two more elaborate cabinets in which a person could be concealed. Such cabinets were designed for contemplated escapes in which it would be impossible for the performer to extricate himself. Houdini's imitators frequently got out of difficult situations by the crude expedient of having a man come up through a trap in the stage, thus entering the cabinet and working on the locks that were on the outside of the container; but his purpose was to avoid anything that would appear so obvious to the committee. He made trapdoors useless by spreading a canvas on the floor, or (in a method to be described) by having the cabinet mounted on a platform.

---

[1] The "plug 8 'fake'" is a special device required to open a type of handcuff known as the "plug 8," which is invulnerable to the usual keys.

FIG. 1

FIG. 2

FIG. 3

TOP—THE BUILT-UP CABINET
BOTTOM—THE PLATFORM CABINET

The simplest method was to have a person concealed in a curtain of the cabinet, all the sides of the cabinet being curtained, and two curtains drawn together at one corner. Houdini's notes mention this, and such a plan has practical effectiveness because of the innocent appearance of the cabinet. It would not do with a large committee on the stage, especially when a close examination of the cabinet was under way.

The *built-up cabinet*, described in the notes, is a cabinet to be built on the stage in the presence of a large committee, and yet to serve as a place in which to conceal an assistant. Inasmuch as this cabinet is of simple construction, it seems, more than any other, to preclude the possibility of a hidden person. The cabinet is large, and rather heavy when completed. Hence it is mounted on rollers, and pushed over the object in which the performer is confined. The cabinet is put together while the committee stands around it; people walk inside and out before the escape is begun. The vital point of this cabinet is a door that opens inward, the hinge being a few feet away from one corner. After the cabinet is finished, the performer invites several persons to enter it and to inspect the interior. As soon as they are in, he pulls the door shut and turns the lock. This amuses the audience as a bit of by-play and causes consternation among those in the cabinet. So the performer finally unlocks the door and pushes it inward; the committee members, glad that the prank is ended, come forth in a hurry.

Among the committee on the stage is a confederate. He is one of the group that enter the cabinet. As soon as the performer closes the door, the confederate, in the darkness, quietly takes his position in the extreme corner of the cabinet. When the door is pushed in, it swings toward the side wall and the man is hidden behind it. His absence is not noticed when the others come out. The open door apparently shows the cabinet still empty. It is left open until the performer is confined; then the cabinet is pushed over the container and an assistant in uniform closes the door. The confederate is then free to do the work. After the escape is finished the cabinet is wheeled back and left on the stage with the door still open. Regarding this type of cabinet the notes state:

"This is positively certain, but you must be sure to have a lot of men volunteer or else one may be missed. In making the cabinet door, have it hinge at least 14 inches from the side wall and thus allow a man ample room to hide."

This is probably the most subtle method ever devised for concealing a person in a cabinet. Its simplicity of operation makes it very effective. One or two extra confederates might prove of use in the cabinet to urge the crowd toward the door and thus keep the hidden man well away from the others. The natural tendency of every one is to get out from in back of the door, and leave the cabinet. The confederate stays there with a purpose.

The *platform cabinet* was a very ingenious method of concealment devised by Houdini. The cabinet consisted of four upright posts supporting a solid top, mounted on a wooden platform. The committee was invited to inspect the cabinet; and it would pass all examination. The assistant was concealed in the top, as in an illusion cabinet; but his hiding-place was rendered very effective, first by using a tall, wide cabinet so that the top had a thin appearance; second, by using a very small person who could fit into an unusually compact space. The height of the cabinet was also designed to prevent committee-men from inspecting the top. Their visual examination would prove satisfactory, and the top being unreachable, they would go no further. The only obstacle would be some agile committee member who might concentrate the attention of the audience on the top by climbing up one of the metal rods that supported it. To overcome this in a subtle manner, the notes specify that the rods should be greased or slightly oiled.

That would end any attempt of a climb the moment it was begun.

The ingenious method for bringing the assistant into the cabinet after the curtains were closed lay in the construction of the bottom part of the top. A long board served as a trap. This was hinged at one end, the other end being fastened so that the assistant could release it with his feet. There were cleats on the upper side of the trap to give it the effectiveness of a ladder. Before the cabinet was brought on the stage, the assistant took his place on the hanging ladder; it was swung up and fastened by an automatic catch. Going up in this position, the assistant required a minimum of space, reducing the necessary thickness of the top to inches. The inside of the top was stocked with tools and keys. As soon as the performer was in the device from which he was to escape and the cabinet was closed, the assistant let the trap swing down so that he could come into the cabinet. Any special tools that he required could be obtained by a trip up the ladder. On releasing the performer, the assistant returned to his hiding-place and was shut in again, with the assistance of the performer. This cabinet is remarkably ingenious, and indicates how Houdini applied all his knowledge of magical principles as possible and useful methods in his work.

The purpose of *assistant cabinets* is very definite. Houdini never intended to use them in ordinary escape work. His regulation cabinet, with its appliances and method for introducing required articles, made it unnecessary for him to carry articles on his person; in a regular type of escape such as the trunk or milk can, he had his own method of concealing necessary instruments. He planned the assistant cabinets for two reasons: one to counteract any unfair method in an open challenge, in which some person might attempt to lock him in cuffs that were "fixed." Such cuffs were ruled out in challenges, but with the assistant in the cabinet, they could be accepted, as the other man could work on them. The second purpose of the assistant cabinet was to make it possible to accept any challenge at any time, without having to devise a method of escape in short order. Houdini planned a milk can that would be entirely unprepared, made of seamless material, or of spun brass. He also considered a glass milk can in which the top could be firmly clamped and locked in place.

From his notes it is clear that he ignored no possible form of restraint. He frequently described a device before evolving a working method that would make a convincing escape. The assistant cabinets offered a plan whereby virtually any type of restraint or container could be conquered when no other solution was available. There is no indication that Houdini ever found it necessary to employ one of these cabinets; but his notes show that he regarded them as both practical and necessary in certain escapes, and because of this they hold an important place among his methods.

Part Two

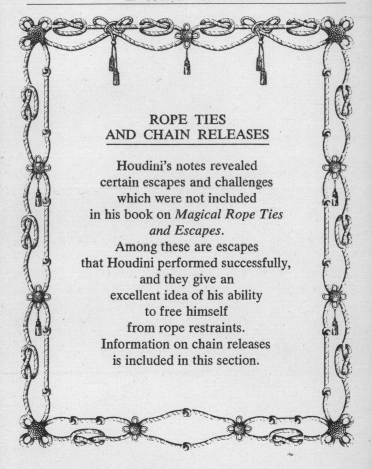

ROPE TIES
AND CHAIN RELEASES

Houdini's notes revealed
certain escapes and challenges
which were not included
in his book on *Magical Rope Ties
and Escapes*.
Among these are escapes
that Houdini performed successfully,
and they give an
excellent idea of his ability
to free himself
from rope restraints.
Information on chain releases
is included in this section.

A special type of rope was designed by Houdini, and is mentioned in his notes, with the statement "great for tying-up purposes." Its usefulness is based on the fact that an ordinary piece of rope will generally pass inspection. The rope is specially made in two sections. One portion has a screw imbedded in the rope; the other section has a socket. When the two portions are fastened together the joining cannot be noticed if the proper type of rope is used, and the ends of the rope may be pulled with no fear of its coming apart. The rope breaks or unscrews by a simple half turn. When locked it may be handled by any one. The performer is tied with the rope around his wrists, with the joining directly above the wrists. By a simple twist he unlocks the rope and releases his hand. He can do this with the wrists alone, or with the aid of his teeth. He can also replace his hands in the rope afterward. This rope serves many useful purposes; it is good for "spiritualistic" tricks in which a quick release and return are necessary. It can also be used in connection with elaborate ties, where several ropes are involved, for the opening of this single rope will start the performer on the road to freedom.

THE SAILOR CHALLENGE

An escape from an eight-foot plank to which he had been tied by a group of sailors was a typical Houdini challenge, and one that required strength and capability.

The notes read as follows:

"I am lashed to an eight-foot plank, with broomstick behind my knees and hands secured at each side.

"Long soft cord or rope is used for fastening the

stick to the knees. I get into a sitting position, the stick is placed behind my knees. The rope is in the center of the stick, and is fastened to the knees; then both my hands are placed under the stick and tied firmly to it.

"I am now laid on the plank, which ought to be at least an inch and a quarter thick, and nearly eleven inches wide so that I can rest easily on my back.

"I am lashed to the plank with heavy rope starting under my arms, crossing over my body and coming back to my neck; the neck is fastened with the same rope, tying it off at the end of the board.

"My feet are now tied together with heavy rope and are tied off at the end of the board.

"There are two methods of release.

"One is to be able to pull the feet out. This can be done with a great deal of effort; if the rope is tied around both feet together it is almost impossible to secure my feet closely.

"When my feet are loose, I can get my mouth to the rope that holds my hands, and untie it with my teeth.

"Second method: After working awhile I can push the stick out from my hands; this will make me virtually loose.

"The articles used are an eight-foot plank; a strong broomstick; and three ropes: one for the hands and knees; one for the feet; and one for the body."

Houdini's description and explanation of this challenge illustrate his individual ability to work himself loose from all forms of ties. It is apparent that certain positions were to his advantage, and that when he gained them he could escape no matter how tightly the ropes were lashed and tied.

THE ROPE PILLORY

This escape is mentioned by Houdini as a good opening effect for a new routine of escapes. It is not a difficult release, but it is convincing and can be performed in full view of the audience. The apparatus used is a T-shaped device—a large post with arms projecting. Each arm holds a ring and each of the performer's wrists is tied to a ring with a double cord. The exact position of the rings is not quite clear in the description of the trick (dated January, 1905). It appears that the hands are tied alongside of the rings, but it is possible that they pass through the rings before the ropes are tied.

In either method the performer can make his escape, and the exact method of placing the hands is a matter for experiment or individual choice, depending somewhat on the size of the rings used. The secret lies in the fact that the rings are larger than the wrists, and the ropes therefore run from the wrists to the rings in opposite directions. This binds each wrist firmly, and the persons who do the tying can satisfy themselves that the hands cannot be slipped from the posts, for any attempt to move a wrist in one direction will tighten the opposite cord. This is the very effect that the performer endeavors to produce, and he emphasizes the fact as the strong feature of the tying.

But the rings enable the performer to slip the cords along the sides and as the cords come closer together on the ring, slack is gained, which enables the escapist to draw his hands free. If the hands are already through the rings, the position is as desired; if they are not through the rings when tied, they must be pushed through the rings in order to take advantage of the slack. The rings must be large enough to permit this, and the manner in which the wrists are tied depends entirely upon which method appears most effective. With the wrists against the rings and not through them, the rings can be set in either a vertical or a horizontal position. The escape is quick and fairly easy, but it has real effectiveness when used as an opening release as Houdini intended it.

THE SELF-TIE

This is an interesting item as it is the opposite of the usual escape trick. It is a rope tie of the type used by fraudulent mediums to prove that they have spirit aid; but in the notes it is listed merely as a trick. The performer enters his cabinet carrying a piece of sash cord about five feet in length. The cabinet is opened a few moments later and the performer is seated on a chair, his wrists and knees tied together so firmly with solid knots that the rope must be cut to release him. This is done with the aid of a duplicate rope, which is already tied. There is a loop at the center—either a single knot or a slip-knot, just large enough to encompass both legs above the knees. Above the slip-knot is a smaller loop just large enough for both wrists, and it is tied with solid knots, which are made tight with short wire nails buried in the rope. These knots may also be glued. As they are impossible of untying, no one will deny their genuineness.

In the cabinet the performer substitutes the original rope for the one that is already tied. The feet are put through the lower loop, with the slip-knot clear up to the solid knots. The large loop is drawn up to the knees; then the small loop is opened and the wrists are inserted. The whole rope is drawn well up above the knees, and becomes tighter the farther it goes. If it does not seem quite tight enough, the knees are moved slightly apart so that the solid knot comes in close contact with the wrists. All this work is accomplished very rapidly. Then the performer calls for the committee, and he is found tied.

This trick is not only interesting and effective in itself; it illustrates a rule that may work both ways. If an escape artist sees to it that his thighs are bound with a slip-knot or single-knot loop, and his wrists tied solidly in a loop above, he can work himself loose, by pushing the cords down over the knees. Outward pressure of the knees is helpful during the tying. This shows the advantage gained by the escape artist who is bound with ropes, whenever he can induce the committee to bind him in a way that appears secure but is really not so secure as it seems.

THE GALLOWS RESTRAINT

As described by Houdini, this is a very formidable restraint, from which release requires special manipulation. It appears from the notes that the first part is performed in the cabinet and the finish is done in full view, the curtains being withdrawn at the performer's call. The performer's feet and neck are incased in straps that have metal rings in them. He takes his position beneath a strong gallows and is secured as follows:

Chains are passed through the rings on the foot straps and are snapped to the posts of the gallows. The chains may be encircled about the feet, the leather straps preventing injury to the performer's ankles. A rope is wound three times about the performer's neck and the ends are secured to the gallows. Here again the strap is important, as it keeps the ropes from choking the performer. A rope is run through the ring in the neck strap and is secured to a ring in the floor. Thus the performer cannot move his head upward. Then the performer's arms are folded and fastened with ropes that are tied in back of his body. Both wrists are against the performer's chest; the notes do not state whether or not straps are used on the wrists; but the ropes holding the arms are fastened at the wrists. There is no possibility of the performer's slipping his hands over his head, as the ropes on the neck would interfere.

This release is quite difficult. The first part of the escape requires a cutter that is close to both wrists. As a knife would be difficult to reach and to use, it is probable that the belt type of cutter is used: namely, a very short knife blade projecting from a belt strapped around the performer's chest. The cutter enables him to release his hands by working the ropes against the blade and cutting as few ropes as are necessary. With his hands free, the performer works on the ropes at the neck. He cannot reach the gallows, and he cannot bend down to release his feet. Therefore he works on the three loops.

As the ropes are not over-tight, because the performer must breathe, he chokes himself temporarily by drawing on one of the loops, thus tightening the other two. This gives sufficient slack to work the single loop over the head. This accomplished, the other loops can be slipped over singly. Freed from above, the performer finds the rest of the escape easy; he works on the rope holding his neck to the floor and releases it; the chains are removed by unsnapping them from the posts of the gallows. Houdini's notes state that the wrists are re-

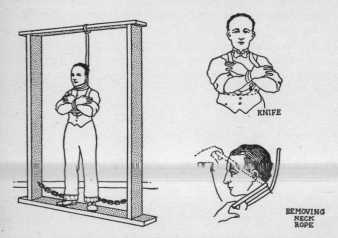

KNIFE

REMOVING
NECK
ROPE

APPEARANCE OF THE GALLOWS RESTRAINT WITH
IMPORTANT DETAILS OF THE ESCAPE

placed so as to finish the escape in full view. This indicates that a cut rope must be replaced, or if straps are used on the wrists, one or both are replaced, the straps being cut instead of the ropes.

When doing the final release in full view the performer makes himself appear as secure as possible, so that the spectators will not realize how much work has already been accomplished.

Houdini also provides for a lock on the neck strap. This can be picked or unlocked; but if a committeeman provides a lock that is unworkable, the neck strap must be cut.

It is then replaced with a duplicate that is prepared so that it can be attached to the lock, to give the appearance of the original strap.

LADDERS AND ROPE CHALLENGE

The Ladders and Rope was a challenge that Houdini accepted on several occasions, and among his notes is a description of the challenge with some instructions for the escape.

The challenge, which is presumably original with its author and therefore the cause of the escape's coming into Houdini's repertoire, reads as follows:

"Harlesden, N.W.,
"October 11th, 1910.
"HOUDINI (The Hippodrome, Willesden, N.W.)
"DEAR SIR,
"Will you submit yourself to a Test I have to propose as follows:—I will furnish three of my strongest

BUILDING WRECKING LADDERS

about 12 to 18 feet in height and laced together in the form of a Tripod; rope your feet or rather your ankles to an iron staple-ring secured to the floor; encircle your neck with rope, knotted, and tie the long ends securely to the top rungs of the ladders. Even with your hands free, you could not untie your feet or neck, but to make assurance doubly sure, I will secure an

IRON BAR OR STEEL TUBE

3 feet in length, behind your back, your elbows encircling same, bringing your hands in front where I will

TIE YOUR WRISTS

in such a position as to render them absolutely useless to you; and will lash different parts of your body to the ladder rungs so that you will be utterly unable to move in any direction whatsoever.

"If you accept, name your night, and I will come upon the Stage with a number of my Employees and test your abilities to the limit.

"You must make the attempt to escape in full view of the audience.

"Yours, etc.

"Signed—HENRY HARVEY

"183 & 187, High Street,

"Harlesden, N.W.

"Wholesale and Retail Building Material Dealer."

Houdini accepted the challenge and made the escape under the conditions imposed, despite the best efforts of the building employees. The trick was so spectacular that he used it on other occasions.

Before we consider his notations on this particular challenge, it should be recalled that the general methods used in rope tie escapes were, of course, used by Houdini in this release. With so much tying, conditions were actually made easier for him; there were sure to be opportunities for obtaining slack.

In his book on *Rope Ties*, Houdini stated: "Strange as it may appear, I have found that the more spectacular the fastening to the eyes of the audience, the less difficult the escape really proves to be."

This applies to the Ladders and Rope Challenge, as the performer has opportunities to shift affairs to his advantage; but the escape presents complications because of the performer's inability to bend his body. Freeing the hands presents difficulties, and with them loose, it is not possible to reach the knots at the feet or above the head.

Houdini made special provision for the release of his feet. His notes read: "Three ladders are used; they are secured together and fastened to the stage so they will not slip. Next my feet are tied with thick rope; this prevents the knots from holding fast, and I can slip from them if required.

"The two ends of the rope are tied into a ring or staple in the stage; I can eventually untie these with my toes after sliding off my shoes."

Houdini's ability to accomplish the feat last mentioned made it possible for him to dispose of any knots on the ring that kept him from slipping his legs free.

His instructions on the tying of the arms were also important:

"A gas piping forty inches in length is placed behind my back; my elbows encircle it. Sash cord is tied about one hand, then to the other; the pipe is secured to my elbows. Care must be taken to make all the ropes encircle the bar or they will deaden my arms and make me helpless.

"Have the wrists tied as low as possible, so they will not pain, whereas if they are tied as high as possible, it will not only make the escape harder, but will cause unbearable pain."

With this mode of tying, the slipping of the bar became an important part of the escape, as it gave slack. With freedom of body motion gained to some degree by the process of freeing the feet, the slipping of the bar could slowly be accomplished.

"The sash cord," stated Houdini, "is so long that one end is tied to the end of the bar and then to the ladder; another rope is taken and eventually two ropes (sash cord) are tying me from the bar to the ladders, back and front. My legs are tied around the knees and back and front lashed to the ladders. The long rope for the neck is encircled about my neck; tied, encircled twice or thrice and tied; then taken up and tied off away from my hands."

Houdini did not neglect measures for obtaining slack in the ropes that were about his neck. Ordinarily this part of the escape would depend upon freeing the feet so the body could be raised, then freeing the arms so the hands could work upward as far as necessary. But he states that the last time he tried the escape, he managed to get his head out first; then by taking off his shoes he untied the knots that held him to the floor, which allowed him to pull his feet free, and after that it was easy sailing.

Without question, this challenge presented unusual difficulties, and all of Houdini's skill and experience were required in the escape. This is evident from his final notation: "In a test like this, if done behind a curtain, it is best to have a knife to cut ropes if necessary." In such an emergency, it would be necessary to cut only one or two of the ropes. The knife would be concealed on the performer's person, under his belt, reachable with one hand. When depending on this method various short lengths of rope are desirable, so that cut ropes will not be noticed afterward. The performer can also hide any very short pieces. The cutting is merely an aid to overcome the difficulties encountered at the start.

As Houdini performed the escape in full view, he never resorted to this expedient. The slipping of the rod from the elbows was the crux of the situation; by forcing it endways, the ropes gradually came free of it and slackened; hence a very formidable obstacle (from the committee's viewpoint) was actually to his advantage.

CHAIN RELEASES

Chain releases are a variety of handcuff escapes, and may be placed in the same category. Houdini's notes include some typewritten material which was evidently intended as part of a separate manuscript, possibly for his book on *Handcuff Escapes*. This describes methods used in chain escapes.

The *chain and lock* is a way of escaping from a chain used instead of handcuffs by police in Europe. The method used by most of the police is to lock the hands crosswise, and from this position it is possible to slip the chain. The performer presents one hand to be chained, and as soon as the chain has encircled the wrist, he lays the other hand on the crossing, and allows the second hand to be encircled also. The chain is then drawn tight, and the lock is attached to two links of the chain. This binds very tightly and appears secure, as the hands cannot reach the lock.

It would not be possible to slip the chain from this position, but it will be noticed that the crossing of the chain makes it form a figure 8 around the wrists. To make the escape, the hands are swung together, inward or outward, according to the position of the chain. When the wrists are parallel, one on the other, the chain takes the shape of a circle, and considerable slack is gained—enough to slide one hand free, and then remove the chain from the other wrist. If the wrists are moistened the slipping is accomplished more easily. It should be noted that bringing the hands together in one direction increases the twist and tightens the chain; in the other direction, the result is the gaining of the required slack.

In the *chain challenge act*, the performer invites persons to come on the stage and chain him, bringing their own locks and using chains that are unprepared and that may be examined.

The committee-men are supplied with chains of various lengths; the performer is bound and the chains are locked, with the padlocks out of reach. Then the performer is placed in his cabinet. He escapes from the chains and brings them out with the locks for a final examination. One method of handling such chains is to slip them. Houdini states that he used a strong pair of hooks, attached to a rope fastened to his foot. After securing the hooks to the chains, it was possible to slip them by foot pressure. He describes this process as being painful at first. Its practicability and usefulness are increased if the performer has managed to obtain an amount of slack while being chained. Chains that could not otherwise be slipped yield when this method is employed. Where chains cannot be slipped, cutting is the method used. This is done with a pair of pliers or wire-cutters that have been concealed in the cabinet.

Since the locks are not in a position where they can be reached, the performer must cut the chain at the most accessible link; when the work has been accomplished, the chain will come free. Obviously the broken chain cannot be exhibited; so the performer removes the locks by picking them, and substitutes a duplicate chain which has been concealed in the cabinet. This is why he must use his own chain; if a committee-man brings a chain it must either be ignored or placed in some position from which the performer can slip it. But the conditions call for the challengers to bring their own locks, as the chains are shown to be without preparation. Therefore the performer seeks to create the impression that he escapes by working on the locks, no matter how inaccessible they may be.

Instead of placing a lock on a duplicate chain and bringing the chain out in its original condition, the performer prefers to appear with the locks open, for that diverts attention from the real secret of the trick—

namely, the chain. So whether the chain is slipped or cut it is policy to pick the lock and show it open, thus apparently proving that the lock was vulnerable despite its inaccessible position. This introduces the obstacle of the committee-man who brings a special lock that is difficult to pick or that the performer cannot pick. The performer, to be consistent, must create the impression that he actually opened this particular lock. He accomplishes this very ingeniously. In the committee is a confederate who is provided with a lock that appears very formidable, but that can be easily opened by the performer either with or without a pick.

After the performer is chained and the chain is fastened with the unpickable lock, the confederate steps forward with *his* lock and insists that it also be used to make the chain absolutely secure. The performer finally complies with this request; the second lock is attached to the chain, and the escape artist goes into his cabinet. Having cut the original chain, he also cuts the links holding the lock that he cannot pick, thus freeing it from the old chain. He then opens the confederate's lock, links it in the closed lock, and brings both locks out in this condition.

These padlocks are handed to the genuine committee-man, and he must use his key to free his lock from the other. The audience observes this. Inasmuch as each lock held the chain separately at the beginning of the act, the inference is that the performer somehow managed to open both of them, otherwise he could not have escaped; and that he linked them together when he brought them out. As the confederate's lock is more imposing, the bona fide committeeman is quite satisfied that his lock was opened, and he wonders how the performer managed to do it. With two locks on the chain, the performer states that the escape will require more time than with one; this allows for the extra time consumed in cutting the genuine lock from the links that hold it.

The *dog chain escape* is very quick, and the method

is extremely simple. Houdini considered it as a possible effect to be used in his new show opening in August, 1905. It appears among notes dated Woolwich, England, January 4, 1905. A long dog chain is examined and wrapped around the performer, binding him securely; then the end links of the chain are padlocked. In full view of the audience, the performer works on the chain and finally frees himself from it.

To the audience it appears that he manages to shake himself free from the chain in some remarkable fashion, and the merit of the trick lies in the fact that it is a quick preliminary to the regular items of the program. The chain is actually faked. One of the end links is insecurely fastened. Houdini's notes state that the chain is examined, but do not specify whether the extra link will pass a quick inspection or whether it is secretly added to the chain after a thorough examination. Either plan is workable. By exerting muscular expansion the performer breaks the faked link, and as the padlock is attached to it, the chain spreads and falls to the floor in a mass. The break in it is not noticeable. Houdini planned to experiment with one chain and with two chains (both faked) to see which mode of presentation was more effective. Chain escapes, as Houdini remarks in his notes, must be worked smartly in order to be convincing.

THE ESCAPE BOARD

This is a highly effective escape which is accomplished by a very simple mechanical device. Houdini describes it briefly in a note dated Detroit, January 18, 1918. The performer is tied to a large board which is constructed from about eighteen narrow boards, set vertically and held together by long cross-braces. There are holes between the narrow boards, placed so that the performer may be tied in a standing position, his wrists,

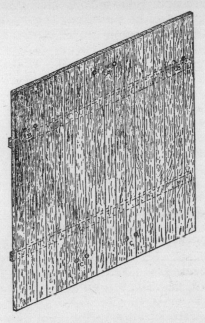

ORIGINAL ILLUSTRATION OF ESCAPE BOARD.
B INDICATES THE UPPER CROSS-BRACE WHICH IS RELEASED
TO SPREAD THE SECTIONS

neck, and ankles being secured by short ropes. He makes his escape from this difficult position. Houdini specified "match lining boards" and stated that by using the feet or unloosening a bolt, the match linings pull apart and thus permit the ropes to be pulled over the boards.

Elsewhere among the notes were finished drawings showing the construction of the board, but no detailed explanation accompanied them. The idea, however, is clear. The bottom holes are below the lower cross-brace; the upper holes, for neck and wrists, are above the upper brace. The trick lies in the upper cross-brace. This is ingeniously constructed and slides a short distance; from the diagrams the end appears to be within easy reach of the performer's hand. The action of loosening this cross-brace spreads the vertical boards, and the performer is able to push the ropes over the top, for the holes are so arranged that each rope goes around a single board. Once the hands and neck are released, the rest of the escape is easy, for the performer can reach down and unfasten his ankles, or can cut the lower ropes if necessary.

The escape board offers great possibilities for clever mechanical construction. Houdini (from his notes) evidently considered a board that would spread at both top and bottom, thus quickening the escape. With special bolts to hold the board so that it would stand close inspection by a committee, it would be quite practical to have the assistants turn the bolts while placing the board in the cabinet, thus reducing the performer's work to the mere action of spreading the boards. This was a method of release that Houdini employed in other escapes; hence it may be considered in this one.

Part Three

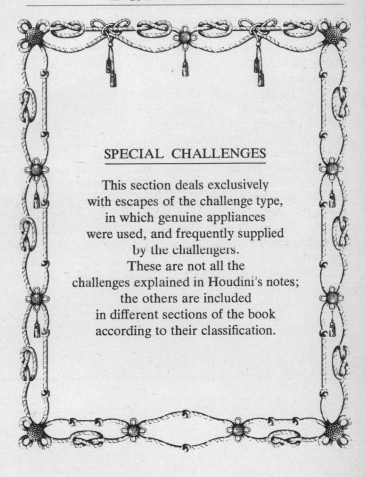

SPECIAL CHALLENGES

This section deals exclusively
with escapes of the challenge type,
in which genuine appliances
were used, and frequently supplied
by the challengers.
These are not all the
challenges explained in Houdini's notes;
the others are included
in different sections of the book
according to their classification.

THE STRAITJACKET ESCAPE

Perhaps the greatest of all Houdini's challenges was the escape from a straitjacket. He performed this spectacular feat before thousands and thousands of people. In the later years of his career, when he did less escape work than before, he still retained the straitjacket, and demonstrated his ability to free himself from the formidable restraint.

The general method of the straitjacket escape is well known, especially as the feat is often performed in full view and the spectators can watch the performer struggle with it. The straitjacket is a device used to bind insane persons who are struggling for freedom, and who try to overcome it by force alone. A sane man, in attempting to escape, can use reason to advantage. In escaping from an ordinary straitjacket, the primary objective is to slip the arms over the head. Both arms are confined in sleeves that terminate in straps, fastened together or to the body of the jacket. If the sleeves are at all loose, the escapist can get his upper arm above his head and finally work himself into a position from which he can undo the buckles of the jacket. But the average performer avoids using a heavy jacket. The difficulty of the escape increases with the efficiency of the jacket, and many who are capable of escaping from some jackets will fail when placed in others.

Houdini, aided by his physical strength, and experienced in this escape, could free himself from regular straitjackets, which were strapped on him by asylum attendants, and in this escape he clearly demonstrated his superiority over those who imitated the feat after he had made it famous. In his most spectacular presentation of the straitjacket escape, Houdini allowed himself to be hung head downward from a building while he effected his release in mid-air. There are a few references to straitjackets in Houdini's notes, and it is quite evident that he considered the possibilities of special jackets for certain escapes. In challenges, regular jackets are usually encountered; but in escapes where the performer supplies his own jacket it is obvious that cleverly concealed preparation is possible, as in other escapes.

Hanging head downward, the sliding of the arms is facilitated rather than handicapped; but reaching all the straps and buckles is a difficult matter. It is claimed that Houdini used a straitjacket in which a hidden bar on the back released the buckles of the straps all together, so that by reaching his back he could free himself. There is good authority for this, but it is not mentioned in the notes. Houdini refers to two special jackets, one with extra long sleeves to help the sliding of the arms when doing the escape in full view. The other is a special release in the end of the sleeve, a strap that can be unhooked by the fingers or cut with a hidden blade. This is for use when the performer is concealed from view, especially when he is straitjacketed in a box or in cramped quarters. The release of the strap is effective, making the remainder of the escape an easy matter; well faked, this device will not be detected, for the straitjacket will stand a close examination, and a careful inspection of the inside end of a sleeve is not an easy matter. Houdini refers to this as the "Bonza" straitjacket in a notation made in Nottingham, on January 12, 1911.

In another note he gives an addition to a straitjacket escape. After the performer is bound in the jacket he is fastened more firmly with heavy sheeting laces so that he cannot move his arms sufficiently to make the escape. The note states that "it is essential to cut the sheeting lace before it can be removed"; hence the escape is made in the cabinet. A special cutter is attached to a post or some part of the cabinet, hidden so that it will not be observed. In the cabinet, the performer leans against the cutter and in this manner severs the laces. This enables him to continue with the escape in the ordinary way; after he is out, the performer can replace the cut laces with new ones. Houdini's note adds that this can be done with two prepared laces, but does not give the details of the arrangement. Prepared laces would eliminate the cutter.

The following description of the release from a regular straitjacket is Houdini's own; it is quoted from his book on *Handcuff Secrets*:

"It [the jacket] is made of strong brown canvas or sail cloth and has a deep leather collar and leather cuffs; these cuffs are sewn up at the ends, making a sort of bag into which each arm is placed; the seams are covered with leather bands, attached to which are leather straps and steel buckles which, when strapped upon a person, fit and buckle up in back. The sleeves of this jacket are made so long that when the arms of the wearer are placed in them and folded across the chest, the leather cuffs of the sleeves, to which are attached straps and buckles, meet at the back of the body, one overlapping the other. The opening of the straitjacket is at the back, where several straps and buckles are sewn which are fastened at the back.

"The first step necessary to free yourself is to place the elbow, which has the continuous hand *under* the opposite elbow, on some solid foundation and by sheer strength exert sufficient force at this elbow so as to force it gradually up towards the head, and by further persistent straining you can eventually force the head under the *lower arm*, which results in bringing both of the encased arms in front of the body.

"Once having freed your arms to such an extent as to get them in front of the body, you can now undo the buckles of the straps of the cuffs with your teeth, after which you open the buckles at the back with your hands, which are still encased in the canvas sleeves, and then you remove the straitjacket from your body."

THE BLANKET RESTRAINT

During the period that he specialized in escape work, Houdini was constantly endeavoring to devise some escape that would take the place of the straitjacket. He regarded variety in escapes as essential to his work, and every feat that proved spectacular made him desire another that would match it. The escape from a blanket of the type used in private asylums seemed suitable for this purpose. His notes on the subject are dated Hull, England, February 1, 1911, and he states: "This idea has been in my mind since Circus Busch, when the asylum attendant related to me about the wet sheet restraints, August or September, 1908." Like the straitjacket, the blanket required a partial freeing of an arm to continue the rest of the work; but it had a wonderful advantage in the fact that the performer's body was entirely out of view during the operation, and the audience's first knowledge that he was gaining success came when the entire apparatus was thrown free.

"This," state Houdini's original notes, "is a regular blanket, strapped around the body in such a manner that the head alone is uncovered.

"The hands are strapped to the sides with straps and buckles. This is done in such a manner that I can always get the hands or one hand free, and can then release the neck straps and struggle out.

"The body is strapped into the blanket, first rolled in, and the straps are fitted around the body: one about the neck, one over the shoulders, one over the hips, one over the knees, and one at the ankles.

"When the blanket is placed on the body, it fits way over the head, but after the neck strap is placed, this portion of the blanket is folded over and makes a sort of collar for the blanket.

"I can figure out a great finish for the escape. By

turning over, I can kick the restraint way off, so I can make a quick get-up for a bow."

Following this preliminary outline of the escape, we read, in capital letters: "THIS CAN BE MADE A GREAT FINISHING OR OPENING TRICK AND IS WORTHY OF TRIAL. THE BEST THING I HAVE EVER THOUGHT OF TO TAKE THE PLACE OF THE STRAIGHTJACKET."

The first detail that occurred to Houdini as presenting difficulties was the matter of releasing the feet. With a hand free, he could work on the buckles through the blanket, and thus attend to all the straps from the neck to the knees. But the escape would have a rather inglorious finish if he could not kick the blanket free, but would have to sit up and deliberately undo the final strap that bound him. To overcome this, Houdini planned a leather-like bottom for the device; this would make it impossible for his feet to be too tightly strapped to prevent escape, for he could gradually slip them free and withdraw them while working on the other straps. Then, with the final release of the neck-strap, he could gradually kick the entire restraint into the air, stripping it from the body and finally pushing it entirely free with a final kick.

Having thus brought the escape to a workable state, Houdini began to plan its actual presentation, in order to make the trick spectacular. The next day (February 2, 1911) he added these notes: "A novel arrangement would be to have the blanket swung between two jacks, so that I would be swinging whilst working. One jack would be at each side of the stage, like those the wire-walkers use, so that all that has to be done is to hook me up first by my head, then by my feet, and I can start in working. If essential, the blanket can be strapped by a ring at each side of the body, with chains leading down to the stage."

Considering the restraint in this form, Houdini made additional plans to make the release an absolute certainty. One was to have the entire apparatus made of leather, thus making it impossible to strap him too tightly, as in the case of the leather bottom for the feet. More important, however, was his alternate method for handling the wrist straps. These, of course, were the key to the entire escape. Hence his final arrangement calls for a special pocket in his clothing, to contain a knife and a duplicate wrist strap. This pocket, of course, is reachable with one hand. The straps proving too tight to slip either hand, the knife is used to cut one strap; from then on the escape proceeds in the usual way; the knife and the cut strap are pushed into the pocket and the duplicate strap is brought out, to be found by the committee after the escape.

The only point on which the notes on the blanket release are at all obscure is the position of the straps, whether they are inside the blanket or not. No diagram appears to show this; but an analysis of the working method indicates that the wrist straps are inside the blanket, binding the performer tightly at the start; then he is rolled in the blanket and all other straps are secured from the outside. Hence the ankle strap goes outside the leather bottom, while the neck strap is out of view because the upper end of the blanket is folded down over it. All operations on the wrist straps are entirely hidden; the others are unbuckled through the cloth, preferably on the side away from the audience. The neck strap is hidden during this operation; the ankle strap is slipped; thus the trick comes to startling conclusion before the spectators are aware that it has reached an advanced stage.

Use of the leather bag suggested by Houdini makes the unbuckling a more difficult undertaking, but this is offset by slackness in the straps, which assists the performer in slipping from the restraint.

ESCAPE FROM A CRAZY CRIB

The escape from a crazy crib is performed in full view of the audience; therefore it serves as a substitute for the straitjacket or the blanket release. The performer is strapped to a common cot, which has been heavily reënforced and provided with loops at the sides through which the straps are passed. Everything may be examined, and committee-men do the strapping. The performer is fastened to the crib as follows: first, a leather belt is placed around his body, buckled, and tied to the sides of the crib with short ropes. Then each ankle is separately strapped to the side of the cot, the performer lying on the crib. Each wrist is placed in a leather cuff, through which a long sash cord is passed; the arms are folded, and the cord is tied firmly to the cot. The performer's neck is fastened down by a leather strap that passes through bars in the end of the crib, and another strap may be secured about his knees. To all appearances he is in a most helpless position; nevertheless he makes his escape.

The full secret, Houdini's notes state, is that the performer is never strapped in a really difficult position. The crazy crib, despite its formidable appearance, is not an unusually strong restraint. The exact procedure of the release is not given; but it depends principally on the position of the arms. As in the straitjacket and certain rope ties, the arms cannot be drawn outward, but the upper arm can slide up toward the neck. This is possible because the wrists are not actually fastened to the sides of the crib; they are attached to cord that is fastened there. With his right arm on top, the performer, by straining to the left, can work his hand close to his head. He cannot slip it over the head because of the neck strap; but it is not difficult for him to reach his neck and work on the strap located there. He then has freedom of motion, which enables him to proceed, once the neck is free. By shifting his body, his hand is enabled to undo the bonds on one side, and from then on the entire escape is merely a matter of continued effort, ending when the performer is in a sitting position, undoing the straps that bind his ankles.

To make the escape more difficult, Houdini suggests that both elbows can be strapped to the body strap by a short strap. This does not interfere with the release of the neck, but it causes difficulty thereafter until the short strap is removed. The performer disposes of the troublesome strap by pushing his arms upward and bending his head forward, so that he can undo the short strap with his teeth. He must do this in order to separate the arms; and unless he is capable of the work, that part of the restraint should be omitted. Any artifice employed by the performer to gain slack while he is being strapped and tied is, of course, to his advantage, and will enable him to make his escape more rapidly.

The release from the crazy crib is highly effective, as the device appears strong and reliable and it looks as though the performer must certainly make very strenuous efforts. Houdini states that the straining at the neck strap makes the test look extraordinarily difficult and that the escape is great for a change—that is, as a substitute for the straitjacket. He adds: "It all depends upon the manner of 'selling.' If it is not 'sold hard,' the test is bad. 'Sold' well, it is great." That is, the escape requires showmanship. Nothing must be neglected to make the performer appear as tightly secured as possible. He must be in a position in which real effort is essential, to convince his audience that the job is not easy.

Therefore the test is only suited to the experienced performer. Houdini could allow the committee-men to strap him to the limit of their ability and to convince themselves as well as the audience that escape was nearly impossible; yet he could also release himself quickly and effectively. An inexperienced performer, on the contrary, would either encounter real difficulties or would perform the test so crudely that it would not excite enthusiasm among the members of the audience. In tests of this nature, Houdini's superiority in showmanship and ability placed him in a class by himself— far above those who sought to imitate his work.

HOT WATER AND WET SHEETS

This was a special test introduced by Houdini, and he classes it as one of the best of all challenges. Houdini was first secured with a piece of cloth tied around his body, holding his hands to his sides. For this test he was dressed in a bathing suit and laid on a sheet placed in the center of the stage. The committee rolled him in the sheet, placed him on another sheet and rolled it about him, and finally used a third sheet as an outer wrapping. Then he was placed upon a strong-framed bed, and his body was encircled by cloth bandages at the head, waist, knees, and feet. The ends of the bandages were secured to irons on the sides of the bed.

The notes made by Houdini specify that the upper bandages should be five yards in length, and the lower bandages four yards; the diagram also shows four additional bandages each three yards in length, running from head to foot at the performer's sides. To make escape from the sheets more difficult, buckets of hot water (about 110 degrees Fahrenheit) were thrown over the sheets, and it was up to Houdini to release himself. This test was genuine; it was very difficult, in fact one of the hardest ever undertaken by Houdini. The only special provision lay in the arrangement of the uppermost bandage which fitted around his neck.

The irons on the bed were placed at intervals so that the distance from the bottom irons to the top was almost the length of Houdini's body. Hence, when the bandages were fastened, beginning with the feet, the bandage at the neck was slanting upward in both directions. This gave Houdini some leeway at the top of the bed, and was of aid to him when he worked his way out of the sheets. His object was to release himself without untying his hands; this he did by literally wriggling from the sheets, a very difficult and strenuous procedure. Once clear of the sheets, he rolled from the bed to the floor, with his hands still tied, and there he slipped the long cloth over his feet and undid the knots with his teeth. As each hand was bound separately and the cloth then circled about the body, this was a task much less difficult than the escape from the sheets.

"This test is so hard," Houdini stated in the notes, "that several times I have had barely enough strength to walk off the stage.

"The committee refuses to allow a silk bathing suit, insisting on cotton, which will not slip as readily as silk."

There is an alternate method of procedure that can be used on occasions when wriggling out seems impossible. The notes read:

"In case the sheets will not allow you to wriggle out, you can, as a last resort, untie your hands, slip them out of the sheets, and undo the knots outside.

"One time I failed to release my hands; so this is a test in which I must actually struggle for freedom with all my strength."

THE MAIL BAG ESCAPE

Houdini, in his notes, classed the mail bag escape as the most genuine challenge he had ever been forced to accept. He appends a copy of a challenge given in Los Angeles, when he was appearing at the Orpheum Theater. The challenge states:

"Houdini will be locked into a leather mail pouch by post office officials. This pouch will be secured with the patent Rotary Government Mail Locks used on registered mail pouches. These locks are made by the government for the sole use of the post office department. They are never allowed out of the possession of postal officials, and their possession or use by others is an offense punishable by fine or imprisonment. The keys are never allowed to leave the post office, and should Houdini fail to release himself he must be taken to the central post office to have the lock opened."

The notebook also contains photographs of the mail pouch, and Houdini marked it as the "greatest test possible in the United States of America," but he did not give an explanation of the method which he used in the challenge.

In other notes he tells the secret of the usual type of mail bag escape, in which a bar is put through the holes in the top of the bag to hold it closed. While this is not Houdini's famous escape, it is a very ingenious trick; for padlocks are placed in holes on the ends of the bar, and the bag is still attached to the bar after the

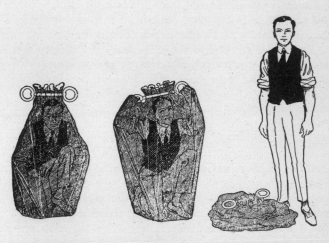

**EXPLANATORY DIAGRAMS OF THE MAIL BAG ESCAPE
SHOWING HOW THE BAR IS UNSCREWED**

escape. This requires a special bar that screws apart. The construction of the bar is so perfect that it is virtually impossible to find the joint when the bar is screwed together; in fact the bar is smooth on its entire surface and may be handled without worry.

The bar is so tightly screwed together that it cannot be separated by the people who examine it; but when padlocks are placed on the end they act as levers, and by gripping them through the bag, the performer can unscrew the bar. When the sections of the bar are drawn apart the bag opens and the performer steps out; then replaces the bar through the holes in the bag. Any locks may be supplied for the trick, and they may be sealed by the committee. A duplicate bar of solid construction is kept by the performer for exhibition purposes. The bars are exchanged before and after the trick.

THE PASTEBOARD BOX ESCAPE

Escaping from a box made of pasteboard would not be at all impressive if the performer merely undertook to break loose from the flimsy cell. But in all regulation escapes, the customary finish is to show the device which held the performer still fastened and secured identically as it was when he was imprisoned. For this reason an escape from a pasteboard box is very convincing, when the committee is allowed to examine everything afterward. In fact such an escape is quite as effective as one from a trunk or packing box, for the audience knows that secret openings or traps are impossible.

In his escapes, Houdini implied that he actually left the device in which he was confined without opening it; this at least was always the indication of the evidence. Hence a flimsy device, which could not apparently be opened without tampering with it, afforded an excellent mystery. It was not a case of strong effort, but of delicate work. The pasteboard box was entirely unprepared; hence it could be made by a challenger, the only condition being that it follow specifications as to size and shape given by the performer. Houdini used this escape, and his explanatory notes are given here.

In presenting this escape, the performer was placed in the box, and a deep cover was put on it. Then the box was bound with ropes like a package, making it impossible for him to reach the knots. Apparently the only way to get out was to demolish the box; but after Houdini made the escape the box was roped as before and stood the closest inspection. Houdini's instructions read:

"The box must be made to your order. My box is generally made about 30 inches high, 24 inches wide, and 37 inches long. The inside is strengthened by a wooden frame. If possible use a dark paper covering, not figured but all black or brown glazed.

"The top must be about 12 inches deep, fitting like a telescope and fitting easily. The top of the box has two spaces cut away, each nine inches deep, and curved, looking as though they were there simply for the hands to take hold of in lifting.

"The ropes must be cut, and for this you must carry a very sharp knife that has an extra long handle. The cutting would be very difficult but for the space at the handles, which makes it fairly easy to cut the ropes from inside the box.

"You may cut all the ropes on the sides, but it has happened the longest rope was unreachable and could not be cut from the side. The only way to beat this is to carry with you a sheet of paper with which the box is covered and some photo paste. Feel along the bottom for the rope and deliberately cut a slot on the bottom edge, and cut until you have cut the rope.

"In challenges where I cut this rope, I try to use cheap cord that resembles sash cord; this cuts easily and can be carried wrapped around the body. But it is best to use as heavy a rope or cord as possible, as it makes the trick appear more difficult.

"The object of having a solid color on the box is so that in case you tear it or have to cut it, you can repair same and this will be almost impossible to detect.

"Once I had to do a new job on the arm-holes as the pasteboard was weak and was badly torn; but I had scissors, paste, and brush, and a sheet of the paper used on the box, and thus repaired the damage.

"The box cannot be moved after you once enter, so the best plan is to allow it to remain on the same spot and move the cabinet over the box.

"Always go into these weak challenges as heavily manacled as possible, as this strengthens the trick."

The reason for keeping the box in one spot is the performer's weight, which makes it impossible to lift the box without breaking it. The instructions do not give the details of the work following the escape, except regarding the repairing of the box, if cut or damaged. But the reference to "sash cord wrapped around the

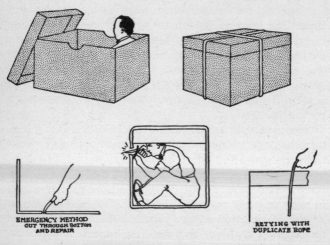

EMERGENCY METHOD
CUT THROUGH BOTTOM
AND REPAIR

RETYING WITH
DUPLICATE ROPE

**THE PASTEBOARD BOX OPEN AND CLOSED.
DIAGRAMS OF ESCAPE**

body" explains this clearly. The performer has duplicate ropes exactly the same as those used on the box. After he is out, he removes the original ropes, and ties up the box with the ropes that he has on his person. The positions of the cut ropes serve as a guide, and the old knots are still there as models when he ties the duplicate ropes. The long rope that may cause trouble is one that has been tied lengthways around the box. This cannot be reached from the sides; to have handles at the ends of the box as well as at the sides would look suspicious. When a single rope is used, as appears to be preferable, it is twisted around the box, going lengthways and sideways. Cutting from the sides, reaching as many ropes as possible, should ordinarily allow the performer to release himself by carefully raising the lid. Additional cutting through the bottom of the box is therefore necessary only in an emergency. Obviously the best type of rope to use is strong rope that is convincing yet easily cut, and that can be carried around the body without bulging. Heavier rope would have to be concealed in the cabinet instead of on the person.

This trick is an excellent challenge, because the performer or his representative can give the specifications for the box and easily obtain a sample of the paper which is to be used in covering it. The sample serves the performer if he needs to make repairs. The type of rope to be used and all other details are decided on before the challenge is made public; this of course is customary.

The escape from the pasteboard box, while simple in method, offers certain complications, and may prove troublesome. The knife must be concealed or smuggled in; also any appliances for undoing handcuffs. The simple procedure of cutting the ropes and supplying others in their place is effective in practice, for no one knows what is going on inside the cabinet, and if the performer removes all evidence and does a good job in replacing the duplicate ropes, no one will even begin to suspect the secret.

THE BASKET ESCAPE

The basket escape is a corollary to the pasteboard box, but presents some interesting variations. It is stronger than the pasteboard box, but the method of escape is quite similar. Houdini's more complete notes on this escape are as follows:

"The easiest basket to escape from is the so-called 'Laundry Basket' made from split elm. This basket has a wooden top and can only be tied with ropes.

"To get out of this, you have two ropes; one you hand to your challengers, the other you have wound about your body.

"They can tie you in, any old way; but the best way is to rehearse them, getting them to tie the basket the same way that the trick trunk is tied: three ropes one way and one the other; this will enable you to retie the basket quicker than will be possible if you have to study out how to retie it.

"You carry a sharp knife with which you can cut the original ropes from the interior of the basket.

"In getting out of a basket that has a lock, accept a basket that you can reach out of at the sides and reach the lock, which you can pick or unlock with a duplicate key.

"Be sure and always try the basket first before having it announced as a challenge. Make conditions to suit yourself. When you have the basket in your dressing-room, you can change the locks or cut off the hinges to suit yourself. But make it dead certain of not holding you."

A notation on the basket trick, dated "Liverpool, England, October 26, 1904," is very brief, and states: "The unprepared basket escape is about the best that can be worked, as the basket is not prepared and all you have to do is to have a duplicate rope and cut the one that encircles the basket; then re-tie the basket with the duplicate rope. This is not as good as being nailed up in the box, but will do for a change."

This is an escape that can unquestionably be made convincing, and the fact that Houdini suggested it as an alternate for a packing box escape is proof of this. A well-constructed basket of large size gives an appearance of solidity. Well roped, it appears secure. While it might be possible to work a thin knife through the weaving of the basket if the weaving yields easily, this is not the method intended for regular use.

The performer seizes the basket by the rim, inside the cover, and draws inward. As the basket is flexible, it bends sufficiently to allow a space between the rim and the inside of the cover. The performer pushes the knife down through the space thus provided and is able to cut the rope without great difficulty. There is no danger of injuring the side of the basket; and, as in the pasteboard

THE BASKET ESCAPE. NOTE CONCEALMENT OF
THE DUPLICATE ROPE

box escape, the audience has no knowledge of the subterfuge whereby a duplicate rope is substituted for the cut original. A very subtle procedure is revealed in the instructions to show the committee-men the best way to tie the basket. Their purpose is to secure the basket as firmly as possible; the performer's suggestion being practical, they invariably follow it, not realizing that they are making an important part of his job easier for the escape artist.

As certain baskets have hasps and staples fitted to them so they may be locked, the consideration of locks in this trick is important. With the handle-holes, a duplicate key, fitted if necessary to an extension rod, can be used. The reference to fixing the hinges is useful in a basket where handle-holes are absent. If the hinges are not already vulnerable, the performer can make them so, and thus open the top without attempting to work the lock. His procedure afterward is to open the lock, fix the hinges as they were, and lock the basket again before encircling it with the duplicate rope.

The performer is sure of the ropes; the only complication lies in locks. If the opportunity is favorable for brief but effective preparation of the top of the basket before the show, any basket may be accepted. The ropes are the important part of the escape. The committee puts the greatest confidence in them; hence the locks are of secondary importance, from the viewpoint of the challengers.

THE PAPER BAG ESCAPE

Like the pasteboard box, the paper bag escape is one that is convincing because the appliance must be handled carefully, and the performer must show it in exactly the same condition after he has made his escape.

Houdini's description reads:

"The bag must be made of stiff, strong paper, and

must be large enough to hold you comfortably so that after you are inside you can raise your hands above your head with ease. My bag is generally 7 feet and 6 inches long and about 40 inches in circumference. You can easily find your required measurement by trying one beforehand.

"In presenting this escape, call attention to the fact that you are not going to destroy the bag; to prove that only one bag is used, you take the bag after the committee has brought it on the stage and allow members of the audience to write their names on it, or to make secret marks; but be careful not to have them too near the top of the bag.

"Come back on the stage, allow yourself to be hand-cuffed, and then enter the bag feet first. The bag is tied with cord, as in the trick trunk bag, and sealed with the challengers' seals. As you cannot move after you are in the bag, they have to pull the cabinet over the bag.

"In from five to ten minutes you escape, and bring out the bag, uninjured and still sealed."

The escape from the paper bag is somewhat similar to the escape from the pasteboard box. The bag is entirely unprepared; but the seal used is a matter of importance. The escape artist must either obtain a duplicate of the seal that the challengers intend to use, or he must see that they are supplied with an ordinary seal. The cord is wrapped around the neck of the bag, and then the seal is applied.

The directions state:

"You make your escape by cutting the cord of the bag with a sharp knife. You must cut through the paper to do this. After you are out, look at the cord and see how many knots have been tied: re-tie the bag; re-seal it with the duplicate seal, using wax that you have taken along.

"As you have furnished the cord for the bag, you have the same length of duplicate cord for re-tying the bag.

"In sealing, use wax matches or tapers that will light

without making a noise. See that your cabinet will not show light from the inside; if it does, line it with black cloth, and when you are re-sealing the bag, place your body so that it will shield the light; that is, toward the front curtain."

In this escape the performer shows the committee-men how to wind the cord around the neck of the bag so he can gauge the number of turns that will be made, and thus be able to duplicate the tie more easily.

The cord fits tightly; and when the bag is re-tied, the duplicate cord covers the hole made in the paper. The cord may be sealed to the bag; the cut is made close to the wax, and the new seal is placed over the old one. This seals the paper at the spot where the cut is made.

Part Four

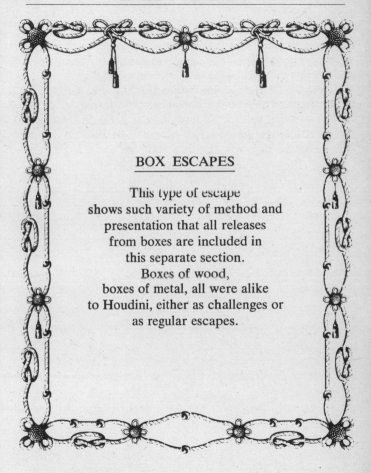

BOX ESCAPES

This type of escape
shows such variety of method and
presentation that all releases
from boxes are included in
this separate section.
Boxes of wood,
boxes of metal, all were alike
to Houdini, either as challenges or
as regular escapes.

Houdini was famous for his escapes from boxes; and his notes are filled with descriptions of various forms of box tricks. Some of these were used by Houdini; others were standard or accepted methods of escaping from a box; while others were ideas or suggested improvements and varied developments. No attempt has been made to distinguish these, as the notes on box escapes do not specify which were used and which were not; but under the general heading of boxes and packing cases there are three important groupings that must be considered.

Houdini performed three types of box escapes: first, spectacular escapes, freeing himself from a box dropped in a river; second, challenges, in which he escaped from a box built and supplied by his challengers; third, routine escapes as part of his regular performances. There are conditions governing each type of escape. In the under-water escape it is essential that a quick-working box or packing case be used; for the performer can take no chances of prolonged delay. In a challenge, the box must be of simple construction, or in accordance with definite specifications, depending upon the conditions of the challenge. In a regular escape, the box that is used must be very convincing in appearance and capable of standing close examination. There are also great possibilities for added effectiveness and additions in the construction of the box: the more formidable it appears and the more complications must apparently be overcome, the more important the escape seems.

For the *under-water escape* Houdini describes a type of box very simple and effective in construction. There are four boards in the end of the box. Two of these are fastened together, but they are not nailed to the sides of the box. They make up the lower half of the end, and

are held securely in place by two concealed hinges at
the bottom, and by two automatic catches that hold fast
to the upper half of the end. These two boards thus
constitute a trap hinged at the bottom and releasable at
the top. The joint between the trap and the board above
is not seen, as the catches are in the edges of the board.
To operate, the performer requires a thin piece of steel
which can be pushed between the trap and the board
above, to push back the catches. The notes suggest an
improvement in the form of an inner slat or brace that
runs horizontally across the end between the solid
board and the trap. This board is held in place by two
screws, and it hides the opening between the trap and
the solid board. Therefore it must be removed to get at
the trap. But Houdini's notes explain that the brace
itself, if attached to the trap, can be made to operate
the catches, by simply unscrewing one screw and pulling
down the end of the brace, using the other screw as a
pivot hinge. The notes suggest using screw-head bolts
instead of screws for more effective operation.

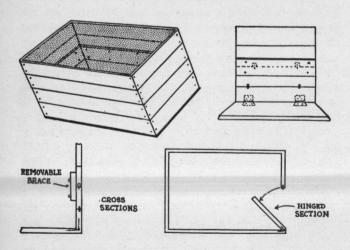

APPEARANCE AND CONSTRUCTION OF THE BOX USED
IN THE ESCAPE FROM UNDER THE WATER

The trap is provided with air-holes; these enable the man in the box to pull it inward, and after he is out of the box he draws back the trap so that the catches hold it fast. The box may be roped; this does not interfere with the escape, for the trap opens inward and there is sufficient space between the ropes to permit the passage of the performer's body. The box remains under water after the escape, and when it is brought up later it is removed from the scene; hence there is no examination of the interior and the brace can remain loose. But it is important to close the opening so that any one seeing the box after the escape will gain no inkling of the secret. The notes do not state that this was the method regularly used by Houdini in his overboard escape. It is probable that he used different types of boxes, and that this was one of them. It will be noticed that this type of escape requires quick operation and certain release. The escape from a box under water is a hazardous undertaking, and nothing can be left to chance.

The *packing box escape* is very similar to the underwater box escape; the only difference from the viewpoint of the spectator is that one is performed on the stage, the other under water. Working in a cabinet, the performer runs no risk, and can utilize a box that will stand close inspection. The inferior method is to use a packing case that opens outward. Such a box cannot be roped or bound too tightly, and it lacks the advantages of a type of packing box described and explained in Houdini's notes. This box requires preparation, but if the box is built to the performer's specifications (as is done in challenges) he can make the alterations quickly and easily. There is always an opportunity for fixing the box, as very few minutes are required and the box will stand inspection afterward.

Houdini explains this method in his notes; the instructions are given briefly on the back of a letter that was written as a challenge, and these notes show how the trick can be performed with a wire-bound box, as follows:

"Wire or steel-banded box. Have the end work. The band-iron is put on with staples, and the board that is the 'gag' falls in as usual, the staples being faked.

"Screws and nails are used; when out, simply put in long screws. To make it look more complicated have staples driven in one way and then reverse. This box is quickly made, easy to work, and looks good. It makes a quick challenge, with no locks required. The box can be put in a long bag; untie from inside."

This explains the working method as a board in one end, held by screws on both sides. The screws are removed from the outside and short screws are put in their place; thus nothing has to be done to the inside of the box. The inside screws hold the board in place

The board is near the bottom, and must be wide enough to allow the performer to get through. The nailing of the top does not interfere with the special board, and the performer's assistants see to it that no troublesome nails are driven through the side where they might interfere with the special board.

To escape, the performer takes out the long screws on the inside and puts in short screws; then removes the board and replaces the outside short screws with long ones so the box will be as solid as before. Airholes can be placed in the ends so as to hold the board in place while inserting the long screws. In banding or wiring the box, genuine staples may be used except on the special board. Any staples placed there must be short ones, hammered in by an assistant or a confederate. A short staple will yield when the performer pulls the board from within. There are not enough wires or bands to interfere with the performer when he comes through the end of the large box.

In his numerous experiments with box escapes, Houdini frequently struck out new ideas. Two of these, applied to the end-working box, are very interesting. One is to have a box tied up in wrapping paper. When the end of the box is opened inward, the end folds of the paper are easily managed so that the performer can feel between and cut or untie the ropes (using the latter method if the box is tied at the end). The other idea is that of a box placed in two bags; both bags are seamless. One bag is slipped over the box and the mouth is tied at the end; the other bag is put on the other way, over the first bag, and is tied at the other end of the box. Getting free from one bag with the knots at the proper end of the box is not difficult, but the second bag appears troublesome. The plan is to use thin bags tied with ordinary knots and to fit the box with panels at both ends. Opening one end, the performer has no trouble with the inner bag. Opening the other end, he unties the knots of the outer bag through the cloth of the inner bag. Then both bags can be manipulated. But even from this point it is a difficult escape, as one bag must be entirely removed from the box to permit the escape through the opening of the other bag.

Special boxes or packing cases, made by the performer or to his order, lend themselves to ingenious methods of manufacture. Various types of boxes are explained in Houdini's notes.

Each corner of the *sliding panel box* consists of upright boards nailed together, forming an angle. The sides of the box are placed within these posts and are nailed or screwed in place. The box stands very close inspection, for all parts are tight-fitting and nothing can be pried loose. No one looking for a trap will find it.

The box opens by a very ingenious arrangement. There are three horizontal boards in each side. One of these boards is attached only to a post at one end. That particular post is attached to no other board or post. The boards above and below the special board have grooves that admit metal slides from the special board. Hence the board and the post at the end will slide away and make an opening through which the performer can escape. Short screws or nails give the appearance of security on the parts that are not fastened, and this device is so neatly constructed that it will stand close examination even if unfastened; thus the performer can

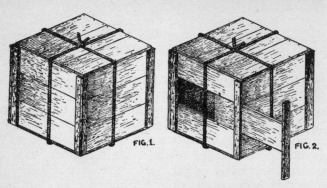

FIG. 1.   FIG. 2.

OPERATION OF SLIDING PANEL BOX

escape from a box of this type without the use of tools.

When the cover is nailed on, care must be taken to prevent any nails from going directly in the top of the corner post. This can be prevented by having the top no larger than the box exclusive of the posts. Secured from the inside with long screws at the end away from the free post, the slide cannot operate until the performer removes the long screws when inside the box. By replacing them with short screws and putting long screws on the outside, he can fasten the slide as firmly as before.

The *telescopic box* is a further development of the box with the sliding panel. The box opens like a drawer. It is difficult to describe but may be understood from the illustration. The telescopic box is an unfinished idea, as it cannot be used in the form shown. The alternate boards and the ends of the frame slide out of the top and sides, which hold the remaining boards. Finished drawings accompany a very brief description of this idea, and it is probable that the artist had a false impression of the trick. In the form illustrated, getting into it would be the mystery. Attaching the center board to the frame work of the top would make the top a separate portion, but would not solve the problem as

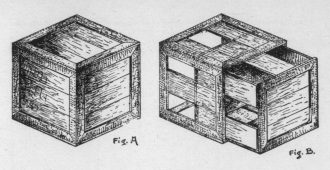

Fig. A

Fig. B.

OPERATION OF TELESCOPIC BOX

the top could be nailed only at the sides and not the ends. A top locking to the sides with staples would be practical, but the lack of attachments on the ends would excite suspicion. The box has been included in the book because it is a very ingenious idea, and can probably be adapted in some practical way. Only a brief typewritten reference accompanied the drawing.

The *slide-up box* is a very useful form of packing box, for it lends itself to adaptations that will be described later. The box is made in two separate sections, one of which slides up from the other. The bottom is attached to the four angle-like posts, which have a framework connecting them. The box itself is made separately, with neither top nor bottom, and slides down into the framework provided for it. The cover is just the size of the inner portion of the box; hence it cannot be nailed to the posts. The performer who is imprisoned in the box merely stands up, and the whole interior section rises with him and may be lifted clear for him to make his escape.

Under certain circumstances it is desirable to have the inner section of the box always loose; being well made, it will not reveal its secret, and no one will be able to lift the inner section easily. With the top in place the performer can exert sufficient pressure to lift

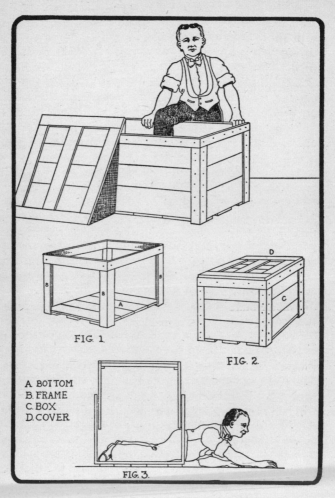

A. BOTTOM
B. FRAME
C. BOX
D. COVER

FIG. 1.

FIG. 2.

FIG. 3.

CONSTRUCTION AND OPERATION
OF THE SLIDE-UP BOX

the box without difficulty; hence a tight fit is desirable.

A few long screws on the inside will make the box absolutely secure. If these are removed and replaced with short ones, the long screws can be transferred to the outside after the escape to make the box positively tight.

It is not necessary for the performer to remove the inner section, as he can make his escape by crawling out between the posts of the frame.

The *metal-rimmed box* is an adaptation of the "slide-up" principle. It is a box constructed without corner posts, made entirely of heavy boards that are bound with angle-shaped strips of metal. The cover is set on the box, and the metal on the upper edge of the box is bent over and nailed in place so that the box is positively secure at the top. The effectiveness of this operation is apparent. The box is made in two separate portions, a top half and a lower half. The metal rim is actually nailed or screwed to the top section, but the lower half is free, provided with dummy heads. Cleats are provided where the metal bands on the sides meet the metal bands of the bottom, and here the bands are separate.

When the escapist pushes upward, the top and half of the box lift, together with all the metal rim except that on the bottom. The rim that runs along the lower edges of the sides and ends is actually attached to the lower section of the box.

The diagrams explaining this trick do not show all the interior details, but it may be assumed that there are pins and sockets in the boards at the broken portion so that the upper half of the box will rest steadily and firmly on the lower part. Nails may be driven freely in the top and part way down the sides, when the box is closed; but they must not continue below the break. The exact position of the break is optional; it may be very near the bottom of the box. Catches holding the two sections are desirable, as they can be sprung by the

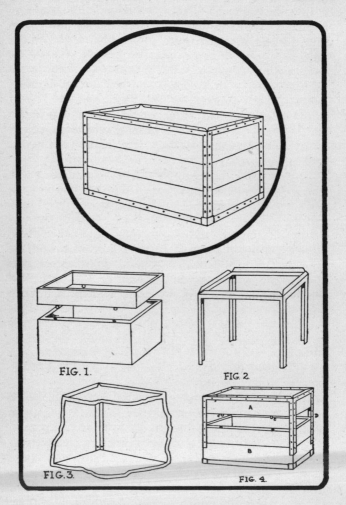

FIG. 1.

FIG. 2.

FIG. 3.

FIG. 4.

DETAILS OF THE METAL-RIMMED BOX

performer when in the box, and arranged to snap back in place when the box is rejoined.

In a development of this box, Houdini suggests an ingenious type of escape. The idea was to have holes drilled in the sides and ends of the box, at the break, these holes appearing between the boards. His hands, feet, and neck could then be roped and the cords pushed out through the holes and held by the committee outside the cabinet. With his hands and feet against the sides of the box, escape would appear impossible. But by merely lifting up and pushing off the upper section, he would automatically free himself from the ropes.

As a feature to be used with the simple metal-rimmed box in which the break is up high and no telescopic cover is used, the rope trick thus described is an exceptional feature that would make a baffling mystery out of an ordinary box escape. The comparatively light weight of the upper section is to the performer's advantage. Adding to the effectiveness of an escape was Houdini's regular procedure. The breaking sections of the metal-rimmed box gave opportunity for a remarkable rope tie, and he did not over-look its possibilities.

THE LEAD SHEETED AND LINED BOX

Houdini's aptitude for improving good ideas and working them into sensational mysteries is seen in this escape. It is a development of the box trick previously described but is so far superior as to be almost unrecognizable. The performer is placed in a box that is unmistakably solid and lined with sheets of lead or iron, the lining riveted together. The outer portion of the box may be banded or rimmed with metal. Instead of an ordinary cover, a telescopic or deeply rimmed top is placed on the metal-lined box. The cover may also have a metal lining as long as spaces are provided for driving nails through it. The object is to have a cover as formidable as possible. The lining of the box is attached to the box itself with bolts or screws with soldered heads so the two portions are firmly fixed together.

This gives the performer three barriers to meet: the sheet-metal lining, the box itself, and finally the cover that fits over; this comes nearly to the bottom of the box and is nailed in every way imaginable. Nails and screws may also be placed in the lower edges and the bottom of the box after the cover is on, so that no escape is possible through the bottom. Houdini refers to the escape as the "incredible" box trick, and the adjective is not an exaggeration. If ever a device seemed a positive prison for a human being, this box would appear its equal. Yet fundamentally it is nothing more than the metal-rimmed box previously described, with substantial improvements.

First the box breaks away at a spot very close to the bottom. The metal rim is desirable for the finish; hence it is considered in the explanation. It is secured to the box at the top edge and down the sides to the break; only the lower portion of each corner band is loose. The bottom band is firm, and is apparently part of the entire rim, the cleats hiding the separation between the corners and the bottom. The sheet-metal lining is very cleverly faked. A piece with turned-up edges is set in the bottom of the box. Then a four-sided lining is inserted; this comes *within* the turned-up edges, so the false bottom is effectively trapped and cannot be removed.

False rivets apparently connect the bottom part of the lining; the rivets that join the perpendicular sheets of metal are genuine. All down the sides are bolts or screws with soldered heads that hold the metal lining to the sides of the box. These are genuine, and they serve to hold the lower and upper portions of the box together; hence the box will stand any test. But as the lower portion of the box is very small, only four bolts

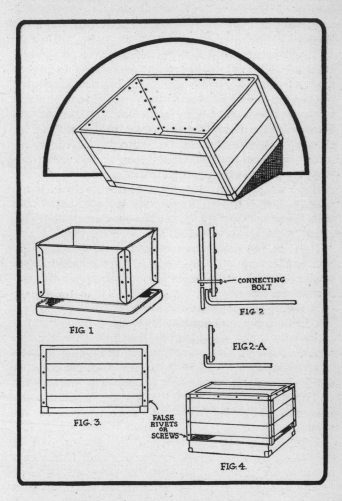

CONNECTING
BOLT

FIG. 1

FIG 2

FIG. 2-A

FIG. 3.

FALSE
RIVETS
OR
SCREWS

FIG. 4.

THE LEAD SHEETED AND LINED BOX

or screws are required to hold it; these are located in the corners of the box. If others are desired for effect, they need be nothing but dummy heads.

When the cover is placed on, it reaches far down the sides of the box, but does not extend below the break. This means that nails can be driven anywhere, in any number. When the performer enters the box he carries some equipment, including an iron for melting solder. He uses this on the bolts or screws that hold the metal lining to the sides of the box. When the solder is off these, it not only loosens them but reveals notches for the insertion of a screw-driver. Thus the performer removes the screws and releases the upper and lower portions of the box. He pushes upward, and off comes the entire top, the upper half of the box, and all the metal lining except the false bottom! He replaces the screws with dummy heads, soldering them in place. All of this is put back in position. As the separate portions are now loose, they must be fastened; here is where the metal rim comes in handy. By inserting genuine screws instead of false ones in the lower part of the corners, the two sections of the box are made fast.

Houdini also provided for roping the box by passing the rope through the handles of the cover and having it so tied that there would be sufficient slack at the bottom to cut the rope when the upper section of the box was raised. This would be aided by tilting the box, but considerable slack would be necessary because the metal lining extends below the break. Airholes in the cover are necessary in this box; they are usual in all such apparatus.

THE DOUBLE BOX ESCAPE

In this spectacular escape, the performer is placed in a large box, which is locked, strapped, and encased in a canvas cover. This box is placed in a larger box, which is also locked, strapped, and laced in a canvas cover. Nevertheless the performer accomplishes his escape and the boxes may be examined before and after the exhibition.

There are three horizontal boards in the back of each box. The middle board is attached to the lower board only by two long, thin metal rods. But for the presence of the top board, the middle board could be lifted from the rods. There are three catches in the upper edge of the middle board. These engage openings in the highest of the three boards. All are spring catches, and they are actuated or operated by a single rod, which is set horizontally in the middle board. An air-hole is drilled just below this rod, at the center, and the performer is provided with a special U-shaped tool. He inserts this in the air hole, pushes upward, and thus releases the catches. This enables him to pull the center board inward and raise it upward, allowing space through which he can pass his body.

With the board of the inner box raised, the performer

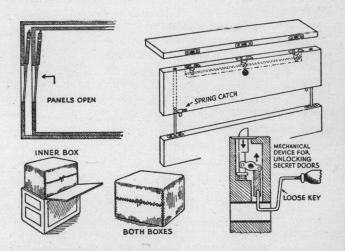

PANELS OPEN

SPRING CATCH

INNER BOX

MECHANICAL DEVICE FOR UNLOCKING SECRET DOORS

LOOSE KEY

BOTH BOXES

DETAILS OF THE DOUBLE BOX ESCAPE.
THE PANELS IN EACH BOX OPERATE IDENTICALLY

loosens the lacing on the canvas cover. The lacing runs horizontally and is properly situated for this work. Much of this is done while the outer box is being locked and laced inside its cover. Then the performer finds the air-hole of the outer box, opens it as he did the inner, and attends to the outer canvas cover. Outside of the boxes, he slides the board of the inner one into place, tightens the canvas cover, closes the special board of the outer box, and relaces the outer cover. His work is then completed.

There must be sufficient space between the inner and outer boxes to allow for the raising of the special board in the outer box, for it must be drawn inward a few inches. The boxes used in this escape must be well constructed, with boards that fit closely together, so that they will stand thorough examination before and after the trick.

This apparatus was constructed and used by Houdini. The escape is most spectacular. Yet the mechanical work allows for a rapid release, and the fact that two boxes are employed makes the effect appear miraculous to the audience. As a regular escape in a regular program, the double box trick is far superior to the ordinary box escape.

THE NIAGARA FALLS ESCAPE

This was merely an idea that Houdini detailed in his notebook; yet it is quite as interesting as many of his actual escapes, for it shows his aptitude for planning the spectacular. The notes state: "The idea is to be nailed in a packing case, thrown over Niagara Falls, and eventually make an escape!" Houdini's plans for this remarkable escape are merely suggestions that had not reached the point of practical solution; he states that it would have to be a trick test, and not an actual escape in the water.

Here is the description:

"So that the crowd can see that I am being nailed into the packing case, the nailing is done on a platform, into which I can slide after the box is nailed up.

"The best way would be to have the platform on a large wagon, which is drawn down to the landing place, where I get into the water according to opportunity.

"Or else get back into the box when placed on wagon, and be found there, having failed to escape (being 'knocked out' coming over falls).

"This can be worked into an extra good idea and needs doing some time."

THE INDIAN BOX MYSTERY

In his notes on the trick he calls the Indian box mystery, Houdini does not give the origin of this unusual title; but he does state the purpose of the escape, namely that it is "to be used on the stage; also made portable to use on steamers or in clubs." The notes were written on August 14, 1910, on board the *Mauretania*. Houdini's purpose was to have a wooden box with a hinged cover, well constructed and strong in appearance, from which he could escape. The sketches show the top of the box with metal bands continuing across as part of the hinges, terminating in hasps on the other end. It is not clear whether the bands were to continue entirely around the box, or to end at the back.

Bands completely encircling the box would probably be used for stage purposes, as the other end of the bands would then terminate in staples to receive the hasps. But Houdini designed this trick with two ideas: first, to make the box portable, so it could be easily carried and screwed together; second, so that it would be necessary to carry only the cover and fit it into any box that might be constructed. In the latter case, especially, the encircling iron bands could not be used, as the size of the box would not be known; in either case, such bands would interfere with the portability of the device.

The box itself was merely part of the proposed mystery. The committee would first strap Houdini in a straitjacket, then chain his legs and place him in the box. Next the men would close the box and put padlocks over the hasps and staples, then rope the box in all directions. The last step would be the addition of a canvas cover, placed over the box and drawn tight, with a rope passing through eyelets in the cover. From the sketches it appears that the end of the rope terminated in a permanent loop, to which a padlock could be attached; hence the rope could not be drawn back through the eyelets. This required a triple escape by Houdini, first from the straitjacket and the leg-irons, second from the locked and roped box, third from the canvas cover.

The escape from the straitjacket was Houdini's first consideration. Inasmuch as space was limited inside the box, he planned a special straitjacket for this escape. The straps coming from the sleeves are used to bind a man's arms to his body; Houdini planned these to release from inside the sleeve, by a firm catch which could be removed by the hand. This made escaping from the jacket very simple, for the arms were freed immediately and allowed an easy method of unbuckling the jacket through the cloth. Out of the jacket, Houdini could easily dispose of the leg-irons; these, he remarks, are to be opened in the regular manner.

The top of the box was to be made in three sections, the center board wider than the others and about ten inches across. These sections were not only fastened together by the outside bands; they were also held together by wooden cleats directly under the bands. The center slat served as a trap. The screws through the iron bands were short, barely entering the wood. The screws through the wooden cleats, however, were long; it was these screws that held the three sections of the box together. The cleats at the sides were provided with long screws, and long screws passed through the bands above the side slats. Removing the long screws from the side slats, when within the box, Houdini would be able to draw in the center slat, or trap. The cleats were not arranged to go clear across the box; their short length made them more easily manageable.

Houdini provided that the rope on the canvas cover should end at the top; hence when the trap was opened, he could spread the canvas sufficiently to push his hand through and pick the lock or undo it. The ropes around the box offered no obstacle, for they were far enough apart for him to pass between them; their purpose was merely to make the box appear more secure. After opening the canvas cover, Houdini's method was to replace the trap. This was to be done without unlocking the box or untying it. Hence short screws were inserted in the ends of the cleats that had formerly been fast, so that the center slat alone held the cleats. These screws were taken from the center of the iron bands. The long screws were then put through the center portions of the iron bands, so that the three slats were held firmly from the outside. This made the trap accessible only from the outside, instead of from the inside, as it had been at the beginning of the escape. Its position was quite as firm as before.

The committee examining the box could not suspect this; for the arrangement made the three slats in the top very tight, and kept the iron bands firm against the box. To all appearances, the top of the box would have to be handled as a single piece, the removal of one slat being the last thing that would occur to any one.

The ropes encircling the box were to be roped double across the top, so that those running lengthwise would pass on either side of the removable slat or trap. This gave the box a very secure appearance, especially to those who naturally examined the entire top of the box as a single piece. A single rope across the top would have been not nearly so convincing; yet it would have interfered with the escape, whereas the double rope did not! For the double rope provided a natural opening that corresponded with the trap itself and could only overlap it to a very slight degree. In making the escape, the double rope proved the least important of the devices used to secure Houdini in the box.

This is an escape that has excellent possibilities, especially for the purpose planned by Houdini. He needed an effective escape that required very little apparatus. A straitjacket, a leg-iron, a canvas cover, and the top of the box (which could be carried in pieces) were the only articles required, with the exception of a few padlocks and tools. It would be a simple matter to have a box made to fit the cover, the staples to be attached by bolts with the nuts on the outside of the box. The cost of the apparatus would be very small. Here again we observe Houdini's ability to build up a highly mystifying act by the combination of several features. The combined effects of the straitjacket, box, and canvas cover make the Indian box a remarkable escape, quite as well suited to the stage as to the special performances for which Houdini actually intended it.

A small diagram in connection with another escape illustrates a box very similar to the one used in the Indian box mystery. Inasmuch as it is through the space between the braces that the performer must escape, the removal of the middle portion of the center slat is all that is actually necessary. In using a box where the cover is nailed on and is not loose as in the Indian box mystery, removal of the entire center slat is impossible.

Hence we find a form of box that is actually a packing case, with three slats in the top and four crosswise wooden cleats, of considerable width, two outside and two inside. The center slat is made in three sections, and the ends of these sections are hidden between the cleats. There are spaces between the ends of the sections. They are held in place by long screws on the inside cleats; the screws on the outside cleats are short.

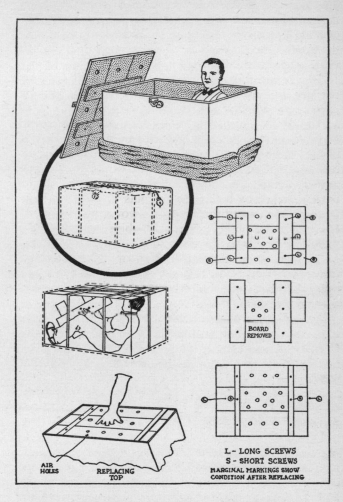

L- LONG SCREWS
S - SHORT SCREWS
MARGINAL MARKINGS SHOW
CONDITION AFTER REPLACING

AIR
HOLES

REPLACING
TOP

BOARD
REMOVED

DETAILS OF THE INDIAN BOX MYSTERY

The middle portion of the center slat is provided with air-holes.

The three sections appear as one, but from the inside of the box the performer makes use of the separations. He removes the long screws from the cleats and puts in short ones; then he pushes the middle section of the center slat toward one end of the box, and thus brings a free end into view. Drawing back the free end enables him to pull the faked section into the box. Having made his escape, he replaces this section from the outside of the box and fastens it in place with long screws on the outside cleats. Note that the long and short screw transposition is necessary only with the middle portion of the center slat.

This method of escape from a box is included here because it is primarily intended for the top and is a variation of the Indian box; actually it is more suited to a packing case, where wooden cleats can be used on both sides and the box must be nailed. Houdini mentions it for the box used in the improved milk can escape; also as a form of release from a packing case. Used with a packing case, it can be applied to the side or the end of the box as well as to the top. It can also be placed on the bottom for use in an under-water escape; in such an escape, the performer would not take the time to put long screws in the outside of the box.

THE BURIED BOX ESCAPE

During the two seasons that Houdini appeared with his full-evening magic show, he demonstrated the test of being buried alive or kept in a box under water during a period of approximately one hour. In doing this, Houdini counteracted the claims of self-styled "miracle workers" who attributed the feat to Oriental parentage plus autohypnosis. Houdini openly declared that the only requisites for this demonstration were self-confidence and endurance, for the air supply in the box used was sufficient to sustain the performer for a period considerably longer than his imprisonment. It is interesting to learn that Houdini considered this trick long before he presented it, and was familiar with the fact that a person could exist for a surprisingly long period of time before his air supply was exhausted. His notes refer to the "buried-alive man secret." The notes read:

"A large box about the size of a large kitchen table. The man enters, his mouth stuffed with cotton, likewise his nostrils.

"He has a hood placed over him, with the eyes cut out; then a longer hood over that which falls over his shoulders.

"He lies down in sand with his arms under his chest; his knees drawn under him. His back is upwards. The secret is that the space made with his knees allows him to have enough air to live fifteen to thirty minutes. Wet damp sand allows longer time. . . .

"When the man takes his place in the bottom of the box there is some sand already, and he is covered with about 1,500 to 3,000 pounds of sand.

"A challenge test is to build a box with rubber band and a cover put on, which is pressed down so as to make it air-tight.

"I presume that with oxygen one could live much longer.

"In the act of lying down, the cotton is pushed out of the mouth; it then lies against the nose in the second hood, which enables the man to breathe."

Knowing that he could breathe comfortably in an empty box—the way in which he eventually demonstrated the feat—Houdini planned a highly spectacular escape, which he describes and explains thus:

"Get nailed into a packing case; lowered into a six-foot hole; then the earth or sand shoveled on same.

"Box can be made to work on side, so that I could worm my way out towards the air.

"Must have the hole in which box is buried large so

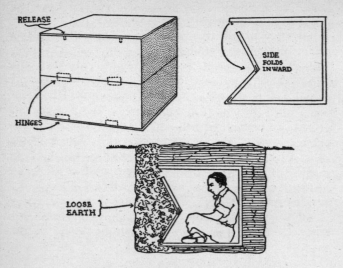

CONSTRUCTION OF THE BOX USED IN
THE BURIED BOX ESCAPE, WITH ARRANGEMENT
OF LOOSE EARTH

that I do not have to strike the solid earth, but can work my way out through the sand or earth that has been dropped on box that contains me. Must be tried out to see how much air I have with me."

Penciled notations follow the typed explanation:

"I tried out 'Buried Alive' in Hollywood, and nearly (?) did it. Very dangerous; the weight of the earth is killing."

Earlier notes on this escape were written by Houdini while on board a North German Lloyd steamer. They are dated "June 14, 1911, near Cherbourg." In these notes he provides for a special type of end trap in the box, which appears to have two loose boards, hinged together and held by a catch at the top of the box. A release of the catch permits the boards to drop inward, one upon the other, thus allowing a large opening for the escape. The notes also provide for bolts to hold the boards in position; when these are released from the inside, the trap is free to work.

Houdini realized that his exit from the box would be but the first part of this difficult escape, and it is obvious that he intended not to be handicapped by any limitations in the trap. Coming out into earth presented a tremendous problem when compared with the familiar escape of emerging into water. In planning his exit from the box and then through loose earth at the sides, Houdini chose the only possible method of escape. Any attempt to raise the cover of the box and the earth above it with a powerful jack would prove hopeless, and there is no indication that Houdini even considered such a method. An escape by raising the cover and thus dislodging the loose earth above would be just about as practical as an exit through the bottom of the box!

THE IRON EXPRESS BOX

The iron express box is a large, heavy box, made entirely of iron with all parts riveted together. Staples are riveted to the front; the hinges are riveted to the back. When the performer is placed in this device and the lid is held to the box by padlocks, the chances of a successful escape seem very remote. The release is effected by simply cutting the rivets at the hinges or at the staples, according to which is the easier. The staple rivets are preferable, for then the box will open in the usual manner; but if the box can be opened by using the staples as hinges, the real hinges may prove the best place to cut if there are fewer rivets there. The box used in the trick is entirely unprepared; it can be of a standard pattern. The escape artist must conceal a pair of cutters on his person and must be sure of his ability to clip the rivets. The box must be unlocked after the escape so that the staples may be replaced. Houdini planned two escapes which operated on the same principle as the iron express box.

The *metal bathtubs* required two small bathtubs with flat rims that could be set one upon the other. These were to be hinged, the performer placed inside, and the tubs secured by straps passing through staples. He also provided that straps could be used all around to hold two separate bathtubs together, the close-fitting rims preventing the use of a knife to cut the straps. The performer simply cut the rivets at the hinges or the staples. The purpose of the leather straps was to counteract the curve of the tubs. Being flexible, the straps would act as hinges where metal clamps would not! and this would obviate the necessity of cutting and replacing all the fastenings.

The *sprinkling wagon escape* was an idea similar to that of the iron express box. The performer was to be placed inside a regular sprinkling wagon, and the cover would then be clamped down and locked. Here again the method was to cut the rivets in the hinge or staple.

THE IRON BOX CHALLENGE

This escape is made from a box of solid iron, the corners and sides being riveted in place. The cover of the box is also made of iron, and fits down over the box itself. Designed as a challenge, this box can be made by any manufacturer or under the auspices of any group of challengers. The box is exactly what it appears to be—a large box of iron that will withstand almost any amount of pressure or hammering. The box itself has no device for locking. It must contain air-holes in the top, as usual in escape devices, and a large hole is drilled in each side near the upper edge, with corresponding holes in the cover.

The sketch provides for four of these holes; one in each side, the box being nearly cubical in shape, and large enough to contain the performer, with allowance for space in which to move. The method of fastening the cover on the box is also convincing. Four solid bolts are used, each with a large head; and these bolts fit into the holes in the sides of the box. The bolts are pushed through from the inside, and the ends that protrude have holes in them so that padlocks may be attached. The box and the bolts are placed on exhibition and any one can satisfy himself that this escape must be impregnable, first because of the strength of the material used, second because of the size and solidity of the bolts. The bolts must necessarily be large so as to allow for holes of sufficient size to receive the padlocks.

When the escape is to be made, the box is brought on the stage; the performer enters it, and the bolts are inserted by the committee members. Then the lid is pressed down on the box; the bolts are pushed through, and the padlocks are attached. There is no possible way for the performer to reach the locks; they are large and of standard pattern, examined or supplied by the chal-

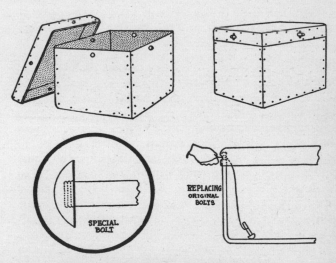

DETAILS OF THE IRON BOX CHALLENGE

lengers. Apparently the performer is in the box to stay. The box is covered with the cabinet, and several minutes pass by; then the curtain opens and the escapist steps out. There is the box, the padlocks still on the bolts. Everything is examined inside and outside, and all is found to be in regular order.

The artifice by which this escape is accomplished is very simple. It depends upon the method by which the cover is fastened to the box, a plan which is specially suited to be of aid to the performer. The only way to hold the cover to the box is by bolts through the holes. This seems fair enough because the bolts are made of iron, like the box, and are of simple, solid construction. The heads of the bolts must be on the inside, so that the locks can be attached on the outside. The heads of the bolts are quite as strong as the box itself. But when the cover is placed on the box, the bolts must be drawn in to allow it to pass. This is done by the performer. When the cover is fitted in place, he pushes the bolts back again.

That is what the committee-men believe he does; actually, when he draws in the bolts, he pulls them all the way in and lays them on the floor of the box. Concealed on his person are four fake bolts, exactly resembling the genuine ones; and these bolts are the ones he pushes out. The difference between the fake bolts and the genuine bolts is this: the fake bolts have heads that unscrew. They are made in two pieces instead of one. As soon as the cabinet is closed over the box, the performer unscrews the heads from the fake bolts, draws them in, and pushes out the free ends. The bolts fall with the padlocks, and the performer is free to lift the cover of the box. The notes on this escape show short chains attached from the box to the padlocks; these serve the ostensible purpose of keeping the padlocks permanently attached to the box; their actual use is to prevent the bolts and padlocks from clattering to the floor when they are pushed out.

The method of replacing the bolts is not given in the

notes on this escape, but this detail is not difficult to supply. By using large holes in the box and cover, strings may be attached to the genuine bolts and passed through the holes in the box and the cover. When the cover is replaced on the box, the strings are drawn, pulling the bolts out again. Then the padlocks are picked or unlocked and are transferred from the fake bolts to the real ones.

THE SHELVED BOX ESCAPE

The shelved box was never built or used by Houdini for escape work, but he invented the trick and gave the idea to another performer, who made a box according to the instructions and used it frequently. The box is an upright cabinet or cupboard made of unpainted wood with a hinged door that opens outward. When the door is closed, a hasp on the door passes over a staple on the side and is held in place by a padlock. The unique feature of the box is a row of shelves that fit in the interior. These shelves go into slides; each shelf consists of two pieces, with semicircular holes in one side.

Three halves of the shelves are pushed into the slides and the performer takes his position in the cabinet. The front halves of the shelves are inserted with the holes inward and the result is that the performer is held in a series of stocks, one at his neck, one at his waist, and one at his ankles. To hold these stocks in position, chains are passed through small holes in the shelves and are locked with padlocks. Then the performer's hands are crossed, chained, and padlocked. Finally the door of the cabinet is shut and locked. As the shelves come against the door, the performer is doubly secured in the stocks, for he could not escape from them by pushing them apart even if the chains were open. The diagram accompanying the explanation of this escape shows all the padlocks beneath the shelves; hence the

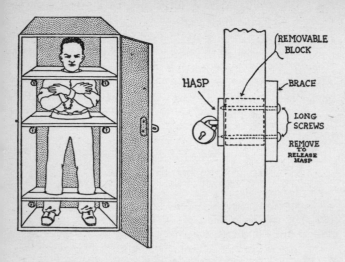

PERFORMER IMPRISONED IN THE SHELVED BOX.
DETAILS OF MECHANISM

only padlocks that are accessible if the hands should be freed are those on the upper shelf. There is no reason why these should not be above the upper shelf, so that they also would be out of reach of the performer's hands. Every part of the apparatus stands close inspection, and its construction is so plain and simple that the device is very convincing in appearance.

In making the escape, the performer first releases his hands, which is not difficult, as they are chained in one of the several manners that enable him to obtain slack and slip his hands. His next step is to open the door; this is done by operating a faked hasp. The hasp is controlled by long screws or rods which pass through a cross-brace on the inside of the door; when his hands are free, the performer draws a screwdriver from his pocket, turns the special screws, and thus pulls the rods out of the way. Then he pushes the door open. The padlocks are reachable and are opened with duplicate keys, or, if mechanical locks are used, they can be opened with the hands alone.

This enables the performer to release himself from the top shelf and the center shelf; with these out of the way he bends down and attends to the bottom shelf. The rest is obvious: he replaces the shelves, opens the outer lock, replaces the hasp, closes the door, and locks it again. This is a very practical escape and the apparatus is both convincing and inexpensively constructed.

THE PLATE GLASS BOX

The escape from a box made of sheets of plate glass was performed by Houdini, and also by Mrs. Houdini. It is an interesting and unusual escape, as the performer, when imprisoned, is visible from every angle. The box is of simple construction. The sides are held together by metal angles; these are held in place by heavy bolts which pass through holes drilled in the glass and in the angles. The bolts are very tight; the heads are on the inside; hence the nuts cannot be undone by any one who is imprisoned in the box. There are two angles for each pair of connecting edges. The cover of the box—also a sheet of plate glass—lies flat on the top of the box proper, and is hinged to one of the long sides of the box. Three hinges are used; they are held in place with bolts, just as the angles are kept in position. The use of three hinges makes the cover fit exactly. The front side of the box has two hinged hasps at the upper edge; the top has two metal staples projecting up at the front edge, held by tight bolts and nuts.

When the performer enters the box, the cover is closed; the hasps are folded down on the top, and large, heavy padlocks are slipped through the staples. The glass box may be thoroughly examined. Washers are used with the bolts in order to protect the glass, but

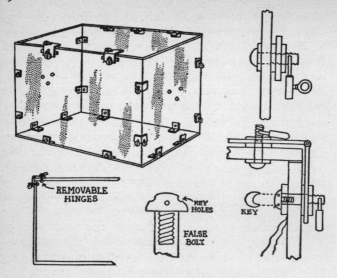

REMOVABLE HINGES

KEY HOLES

FALSE BOLT

KEY

THE PLATE GLASS BOX. NOTE HOW THE BOLTS
ARE LOCKED. THE DIAGRAMS SHOW CONSTRUCTION
OF THE FALSE BOLTS

there is no deception about them. The fact that plate
glass is used makes any hidden mechanism an impos-
sibility. Any person can satisfy himself that the box is
without preparation, and an inspection can be made in
a very few minutes. Yet the performer escapes from the
crystal casket a few minutes after the cabinet is placed
over it, and the box is found to be as firmly locked as
ever.

The secret of the escape lies in the hinges. These are
not faked, but the bolts through the back of the box are
of special construction. Each bolt is large and consists
of two portions, the bolt itself, which is hollow at one
end, and the bolt-head, which is provided with a small
screw-bolt. When the bolt-head is screwed into the hollow end of the bolt (which is threaded to receive it),
the result is apparently a solid bolt that exactly resembles the real bolts used on all the other parts of the

glass box. From inside the box, the performer can unscrew the bolt-heads, push the bolts out of the holes, lift up the cover with the hasps acting as hinges, and thus make an escape.

So that the bolts may pass the most rigid inspection, the heads are screwed in so tightly that they cannot be removed except by the use of a special tool. One method of accomplishing this is with bolts that have small holes in the solid heads. The holes are short depressions that do not extend deep into the heads. The performer has a flat key, with extending prongs, which are pushed into the holes of each bolt-head; the key is turned, and the bolt-head is quickly and easily unscrewed. After the escape, the replacement of the special bolts is not a difficult matter. The heads are put back in place, and the nuts are removed. The bolts may be attached to cords which are passed through the holes in the glass so that the bolts may be drawn into position from within the box and the nuts replaced. But if the padlocks are the performer's own or are of a type which may be easily opened, the simplest method is to unlock them, releasing the front of the cover, and thus replace the bolts in the hinges. The cover may then be closed and relocked. Another method is to tilt the box backward, slip the bolts through the holes in the back, and fit the hinges over the ends of the bolts, after which the nuts may be tightened from the outside. It is quite an easy matter to substitute genuine bolts for the special bolts after the escape. The extra bolts may be concealed in the cabinet. This will allow the glass box to be examined with no possibility of any one's discovering the secret.

The only article which the performer must carry into the box is the small flat key, which may be concealed without any difficulty. There are no less than forty-two bolts used in the plate glass box. These are all exactly alike in appearance. All but three of them are genuine. With so many bolts to examine, and without the special tool at their disposal, the committee-men have no opportunity to discover anything amiss. Suspicious committee-men naturally direct their attention to the hasps and staples of the box. The bolts used there are genuine; that is a subtle feature of the trick. Opening the cover from the hinge side is an excellent procedure. The plate glass box is an ingenious escape, because its secret is so effectively protected. It is effective because it is quickly and easily accomplished and affords no complications. It is convincing to both the audience and the committee because of its simple construction that permits a view of the interior after the box is closed.

Part Five

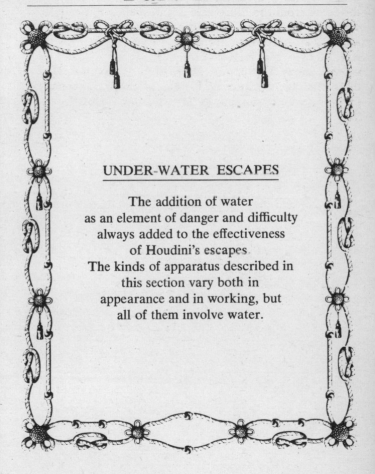

UNDER-WATER ESCAPES

The addition of water
as an element of danger and difficulty
always added to the effectiveness
of Houdini's escapes.
The kinds of apparatus described in
this section vary both in
appearance and in working, but
all of them involve water.

RUBBER BAG· AND GLASS BOX

Of all the escapes explained in Houdini's notes, the rubber bag and glass box most aptly proves that a very simple trick can be made into a spectacular mystery if properly presented. Everything in this trick is designed to mislead the audience. The objects that are used seem free of trickery because of their construction. It appears that the escape must require a long time to accomplish, whereas it is very quick; and finally, the escape seems to be full of complications, while actually it is comparatively easy of execution.

The conditions under which the performer is imprisoned are novel and unusual. He is placed in a bag made entirely of rubber, which will pass close examination. Then the top of the bag is tied with rope and knotted by members of the committee. In the sides of the rubber bag are two small holes; these are fitted with valves, so that two long pieces of rubber hose may be attached. A water-tight box is then required. The committee has been examining this, and the inspection shows that it is a glass aquarium with wooden posts and bottom, sheets of glass set in a wooden frame with a hinged top provided with a hasp and staple at the other side.

The bag containing the performer is placed in the glass box, and water is introduced with a fire-hose. As soon as the water reaches a point above the bag, an assistant begins to let oxygen into one hose from a tank; the other hose passes off to a post, and allows bad air to escape. The cover has two cut-outs, one on each side, so that when the glass box is filled with water and the top is closed, nothing interferes with the rubber hose. Then the box is padlocked, and the cabinet covers the box, leaving the assistant with the oxygen tank outside.

By this time the audience is deeply interested. Here is a double problem. The performer must escape from the rubber bag and then make his exit from the box. Meanwhile he is dependent on the hose for air. To escape from the bag first will leave him without his air supply, and he may not have time to work free from the box; to escape from the box first seems quite impossible, for the rubber bag interferes with the performer's actions.

Yet that is the way he intends to go about it. For when the curtains are thrown aside, the performer is not only free but dry. The glass box is locked and may be examined; the rubber bag is inside, still knotted, and puffed with air!

From the standpoint of presentation, this trick is excellent. It is one that people will talk about; it is therefore a real box office attraction. Furthermore the man who does it has a much easier task than the audience supposes, and to a performer of Houdini's ability, the trick would be nothing more than a simple routine. At the same time, this is an escape designed for a showman, and Houdini's extensive notes on the trick prove that he recognized its great possibilities.

Analyzing this escape, we observe that the performer must release himself from the glass box before attending to the rubber bag. The release from the box must be sure and easy, yet well concealed, for the performer is unquestionably handicapped by being in the bag. Hence Houdini states that the top must come up away from the frame so that by simply standing up, the cover is raised. "This," he wrote, "can be cleverly concealed" in the following manners:

First Method. The glass is attached to the top by a brass binding which is heavy at the corners; that is, the glass simply rests on the wooden frame, and the brass holds it in position. Bolts pass through the brass and enter the wood. These bolts go into holes that have been made in the wood. Hence the glass is held firmly to the top, but the bolts are removable. They appear to serve the purpose of screws, fastened into the wood itself. The top thus stands careful examination, especially as the spectators in the committee are devoting most of their attention to the lower part of the frame, where it fits on the framework of the box.

There is no indication of the bolts inside the box; they cannot be operated from there; hence no one worries about them. The persons examining the box are easily convinced that the glass part is firmly in place. The performer cannot reach the outside of the box. This is where the assistants play an important part. It is necessary for them to move the box slightly so that the cabinet may be set on it. They naturally take hold of the top corners of the box, and their fingers finding the bolts draw the bits of iron back from the wooden holes. The bolts, it may be observed, are not necessarily removable. They cannot come all the way out. Slots from the brass binding down will enable them to slide up with the binding when the ends of the bolts do not engage the holes that are deep in the woodwork.

There may be several bolts at each corner; all may work free (either by slots or by faked bolt heads) except one key bolt at each corner; these hold the glass and the binding firmly enough to pass inspection. Thus when the performer stands up in the rubber bag, he can lift off the glass and its broad brass binding and carefully set it alongside of the box, using his hands through the rubber bag.

Second Method. This release is in the hasp on the outside of the box. The staple is on the box; the hasp portion is on the cover. There are no inside connections, but the staple itself is operated in a neat mechanical fashion. Pulling on it will not disengage it from the box; *spreading* it will do the trick. Instead of using a padlock, an examined bolt and nut are used to hold the hasp to the staple. These are placed in position. The bolt is wedge-shaped, and is forced down tight by an assistant. This makes the fastening appear secure; it also spreads the staple automatically, and when the performer presses against the top of the box, the staple comes out, allowing the cover to be raised.

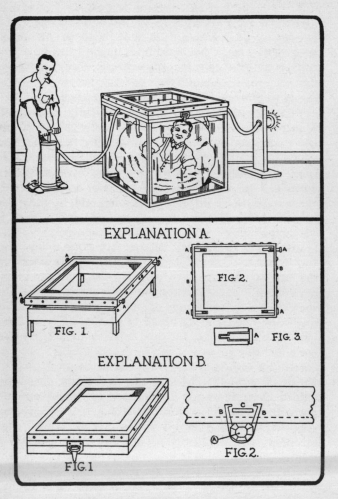

EXPLANATION A.

FIG. 1.

FIG. 2.

FIG. 3.

EXPLANATION B.

FIG. 1

FIG. 2.

THE RUBBER BAG AND GLASS BOX

Thus the entire cover of the box is solid and will stand any amount of examination; after the performer is out, a slight loosening of the bolt allows him to put the staple back in its original position. An alternate type of staple is a metal fitting that goes in the woodwork of the box. This is held by strong springs or fastenings, and ordinary pulling will not remove it. When the performer presses firmly against the front of the cover, he pulls the staple clear of the woodwork.

Third Method. This plan, which Houdini considered probably the best, reverts to the extreme top of the cover—where the glass is bound into the box. The binding is held to the woodwork by hidden catches set in the woodwork. Bolts or screws through the binding either are free in the wood (by slots) or do not enter it. Yet the catches hold the binding securely, and there is no way in which they can be discovered or removed by the committee. These catches are actuated by little levers in the woodwork; the levers are horizontal and end in plugs set in vertical holes. On the framework of the box are pins that correspond with these holes. The obvious purpose of the pins and holes is to set the cover squarely on the box and hold it there so that padlocks may be attached to hasps and staples on all sides. Everything undergoes a rigid examination before the trick, for the glass and its framework are actually secure to the top of the cover. But as soon as the cover is fitted into position, the pins automatically operate the hidden catches, and the glass and framework may be pushed upward. The framework should be a tight fit, requiring a certain amount of pressure to free it. After escaping, the performer simply puts the glass and framework on again. As soon as the cabinet is removed, the locks are examined and taken off; then the assistants lift the cover and offer it for another examination. The catches having springs are back in their original position, and the entire top is in perfect condition.

The Bag Escape. Escaping from the bag is an important item; the performer accomplishes this by untying the knots through the bag itself. The bag is made of thin rubber, and the knots can be very effectively handled. Houdini made little mention of this item, for untying knots through cloth or rubber offered him no difficulty. The supplying of a short length of rope makes it impossible to tie intricate knots, and the performer can retie the bag after he is out of it. Yet the use of the bag is extremely effective, especially because of the water. It makes a good box trick into an extraordinary one, and the bag escape and tank escape are an excellent combination when worked together.

Of course the performer does not replace the parts of the glass box until he has released himself from the bag. He puts the bag into the box before making the box as secure as in the beginning, and being free from the bag, he has no difficult operations. It is also essential that the bag should be tied in a regular manner so that no difference will be detected by the committee; furthermore, the knots are wet and are not so easy to handle as dry knots. But well tied with square-knots, the bag will unfailingly satisfy the usual stage committee. As the preparations for the trick are rather elaborate and lengthy, the time allowed for this work is too short to permit delayed tying. In an emergency the performer may simply cut the rope with a sharp-pointed instrument and replace the old one with a new rope, covering the small opening in the rubber; or he can destroy the bag itself by cutting it or ripping it, replacing it with another bag tied exactly like the original. A duplicate bag and rope are therefore items of equipment to be concealed in the performer's cabinet.

THE CRYSTAL WATER CASKET

This is one of the most spectacular of all escapes. Consider a man imprisoned in a massive casket entirely filled with water and secured from the outside with genuine locks and massive straps, the walls and top of the casket made of glass! The escape must be effected within a very few minutes, and escape seems impossible, for alert committee-men may examine and seal the contrivance. Yet Houdini not only planned such a formidable device; he devised an ingenious method of getting out of it. The casket as the audience sees it is a strong wooden framework that supports sides of clear glass. A heavy cover fits on the casket; the sides of the cover are of glass, and so is the top. Both parts may be carefully inspected. Brass trimmings are on the edges, and the casket and cover are water-tight. There is a certain peculiarity of the cover that serves a definite purpose. The sheet of glass on the top has a hole in the center. This hole is bound with metal and connected to the brass rim of the cover by flat bars both above and below the glass.

The casket is filled with water, and the performer appears in a bathing suit. Then he enters the casket and stands there with his head and shoulders out of water. The cover is lifted and set on the casket. It has a close-fitting downward flange that goes over the top edges of the casket and makes the whole affair water-tight. Each side of the cover is supplied with a large mechanical lock which operates perfectly. These locks are thoroughly examined by the committee, and they pass inspection. They are inaccessible from within the cabinet. But to render the contrivance doubly secure, there are two staples on each side of the cover and corresponding staples on each side of the casket. As these staples are horizontal, the committee-men can run heavy straps through them. Thus there are four straps, two in each direction, passing over and under the casket, which is mounted slightly to permit the passage of the straps. No effort is spared to make these straps tight, and they are buckled at the bottom of the cabinet. Their purpose is evident. Should the locks fail to hold the cover, the straps would still be an insurmountable barrier. For the lip or flange of the cover is too deep to allow the performer to reach through by pressing the cover upward. The heavy straps are virtually unyielding; pressure can stretch them but the fraction of an inch. The only opening into the casket is the hole in the center of the cover; it is so small that the performer can merely put his arm through. But a hemispherical cap is designed to fit over it, and this fastens down to solid bolts or clamps that are thoroughly inspected and approved by the committee.

When the escapist is in the casket and the cover is on with the straps and locks firmly secured, a funnel is inserted in the small hole in the center of the top, and water is poured in through a hose. The closed casket is water-tight; hence the water-level rises, and the performer, who has moved to a corner, is entirely immersed, with no possibility of obtaining air, for the water comes to the very top. Then the hemispherical cover is clamped on the hole; the bolts or clamps work quickly, so that the prison is sealed with a few seconds. Curtains are drawn about the apparatus, and the audience realizes that the performer is in a most precarious position. Three or four minutes seem the maximum time permissible for this escape, due to the lack of air within the casket; and the performer has lost a few precious seconds in the closing of the hole in the top. As the minutes go by, the spectators become tense and wonder what is going on inside the curtains. For this escape carries a real element of danger. Suddenly the curtains are thrown aside and there stands the performer, dripping with water. The casket is still locked and strapped; the water-level has dropped because the performer is no longer within. The committee steps forward to inspect the apparatus. Nothing has been changed; everything is secure. The casket may be opened if desired, and an inspection of the interior will show nothing amiss. There is a certain similarity between the crystal water casket and the glass box from which the performer escapes while in a rubber bag. But in the crystal casket, quick escape is much more essential, and the apparatus is much heavier and more formidable. The first thing to consider is the spot where the performer makes his exit. This is at the extreme top of the cover. As in the glass box, the glass lifts off with the brass binding. This part of the apparatus must be secure when the committee examines it; yet it must be capable of quick release. The first method used in the glass box can be applied to the crystal casket also. A loose brass binding, held with bolts that fit in holes and draw back to slots, will serve. These bolts are in the corners and are withdrawn by the assistants while moving the casket. But it is not the ideal arrangement, first because there is no excuse for delay, second because the casket is very heavy and cannot well be moved. The curtains are placed around it or a cabinet lowered over it.

So Houdini planned a special release for the interior, and while his diagrams are lacking in mechanical details, they at least give the fundamental idea of the method he devised. There are hidden catches in the center of each portion of brass framework. The framework is enlarged at these points, because it connects with the hole in the center of the top. The diagrams indicate a single release for each of these catches, operating from the center of the top. This appears to be a twist of the center rim, giving a corresponding turn to the flat rods extending to the brass framework. The rods operating thus are the ones beneath the glass. One arrangement would be for this to turn or operate by moving the cap itself, and it is possible to have the turning take place only when the cap is in position; it is simpler, however, to have everything take place from beneath, in which case the rods can move independently, each being operated individually from a position at the center. Their release may also depend on pressure from pins used to set the cap in place.

These details, while based on a study of Houdini's sketches, are speculative; the important point is that he

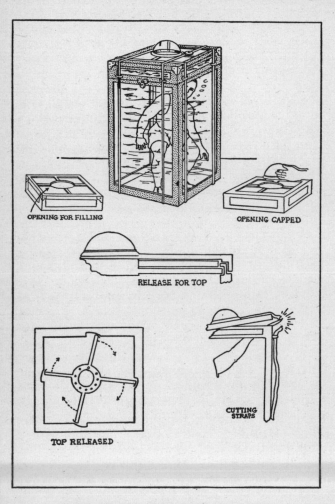

OPENING FOR FILLING

OPENING CAPPED

RELEASE FOR TOP

TOP RELEASED

CUTTING STRAPS

DETAILS OF THE CRYSTAL WATER CASKET

regarded such a release as being not only practical but also undetectable and preferable to any other. If his plans had proven unsatisfactory, the release used in the glass box could have been applied to the crystal casket also. There are three factors in addition to its mechanical perfection that guard the secret of the release. First, there is much to be done and inspection is sure to be brief: second, every one looks for trickery at the spot where the cover joins the casket, so that attention is centered there; third, the straps seem to preclude all possibility of any mechanical arrangement. It is these straps which are our next consideration. Having released the top of the cover, what can the performer do? The straps are not faked, and he is still in the cabinet.

The brass binding offers the solution. It is not wide except at the corners and at the middle points where it joins with the strips or rods that go to the center of the top. In those spots it is apparently fastened to the woodwork, but the bolts are fakes or short bolts that fit in slots in the wood. Between the middle points and the corners, the binding does not come far below the glass. Now the straps will give, no matter how tightly they are fastened. They will not yield sufficiently to be of any use at the bottom of the cover, where the overhanging edge is thick and deep to make the casket entirely watertight; but at the binding only a little stretching is necessary to enable the performer to insert a thin-bladed knife between the binding and the woodwork. The straps pass by spots where the binding is not deep, and the knife can be worked through when the performer presses upward on the top of the cover.

Thus he cuts all four straps; then he lifts the top of the cover and leaves the box. There is one important point, however, which must not be overlooked. The performer has released the top; he has cut the straps; but what has he done for air in the meantime? He certainly cannot count on finishing operations on the straps before he is out of breath. The answer to this problem is found in the hemispherical cover that fits over the center of the top. It contains air; and when the performer needs a fresh supply, he goes back to it. The cap is smaller than his head; hence its purpose is not suspected. The performer gets the air by tilting his head backward so that his nose and mouth come out of the water! Houdini evidently estimated that the few breaths the performer would require were contained within the cap, but he also had an emergency measure in case the cap should prove too small for its required purpose. That was to have the bottom of the cap slightly faulty, so that when it was clamped down it could never lie absolutely flat on the rim beneath. As a result the cap would not be air-tight, and the performer's air supply could last almost indefinitely.

Once out of the casket, the performer's task is to remove the cut straps and replace them with duplicates hidden in the cabinet covering the casket. He must also replace the catches so that the top of the cover will be firmly in position. That is why a turn of the cap is desirable, for the catches can then be thrown back from the outside of the casket. If such a mechanism is too complicated and the catches must be handled from inside the cover, the performer must unlock the locks, remove the cover, and fit the top portion into position. The locks, while genuine, are part of the casket, so that duplicate keys are easily retained by the performer. No water will come from the casket when the top is removed, for the performer's body has displaced a considerable quantity, and the level will normally be below the upper edge of the casket. If the glass box type of release is used (i.e. a release from outside the cabinet) the performer's task is simplified, as he has merely to undo the simple action of his assistants before the escape.

To the audience the crystal water casket is a sensational escape in which the odds are so greatly against the performer that his act of freeing himself seems miraculous. To the performer it is a workable device that requires nerve and ability but is well worth it because of its effectiveness. Houdini, with his fearlessness and strength, his ability and his experience, could attempt escapes of this caliber and present them successfully where others would have hesitated and eventually abandoned the idea.

A GLASS CABINET

This method of escaping from a glass cabinet of simple construction is not one of Houdini's originations; it was given to him by the designer, and it is quite obviously inferior to the escapes created by Houdini. It involves, however, a novel use for padlocks of special construction.

The trick requires a glass case or cabinet taller than the performer and made entirely of glass. This would probably need a metal bottom and reënforced sides, as the glass cabinet is to hold water. There are two holes in each side of the cabinet; these are just below the top edge, making eight holes in all. The performer is imprisoned in the cabinet by the simple process of covering it with a sheet of glass which has holes drilled in the edges close to the holes in the cabinet. Eight padlocks are used. These are tested beforehand, and as soon as the performer is under the lid of the cabinet the locks are slipped into place, each lock going through a hole in the cabinet and a hole in the sheet of glass.

As the time element is important, with water in the cabinet, self-locking padlocks are used. They are snapped into place quickly, and curtains are placed over the glass cabinet. The trick lies in the padlocks. These are double-acting. Pressure on a knob or center point on the arm of one of these locks releases it. The performer presses all the locks, slips them from the holes, and lifts the sheet of glass. Coming out of the cabinet, he replaces the sheet of glass and snaps the locks back in place.

With eight locks, the time required to escape would be to the performer's disadvantage unless the cabinet contained some air. Four would be preferable if the cabinet were entirely filled with water. The real merit of the trick lies in the fact that these locks can be neither unlocked nor picked, for the key-holes, hinges, and clasps are impossible to reach. Performed without the use of water, it would make a sure and effective escape.

THE SUBMERGED TRUNK ESCAPE

The mystery of the submerged trunk was devised by Houdini in 1909, or before; his complete notations and sketches are dated Croydon, England, September 9, 1909. It is one of those rare escapes that carry a double mystery, and it illustrates Houdini's capability for making a seemingly miraculous effect out of a rather hackneyed trick. For with the submerged trunk, the escape seems unbelievable even after it has been accomplished. The trunk used in the escape is large and solidly made. It possesses no air-holes; on the contrary it must be made air-tight, so that it may be submerged in a tank of water. This tank has a glass front; after the performer is locked in the trunk, his air-tight prison is lifted and lowered into the tank, where it is completely under water. Then the curtain is drawn around the tank.

It is obvious that the performer must escape quickly. The trunk has been hurriedly locked and roped, and the expectant audience realizes that no time must be lost, because of the limited supply of air. This adds to the tenseness of the situation. After several minutes have passed, the curtain opens and out steps the performer. He has made the escape, but to the amazement of the audience he is as dry as when he entered the trunk! The cabinet is removed, and everything undergoes the most rigid examination. The trunk is still in the tank, under water. It is lifted from the tank and inspected; the locks are still fastened, and the ropes are intact. The trunk is opened, and the interior is shown to be quite dry.

This bewildering effect is particularly good from the magician's standpoint, for it offers a variety of impractical solutions, all of which, like the trunk, do not hold water. "An optical illusion"—"duplicate trunks"—"the performer is never in the trunk"—"the tank empties and refills itself"—these are the theories that will occur to members of the committee on the stage; yet they will find no evidence to support any of these pet beliefs. This is indeed an escape that can create amazement. Yet the secret is very simple; in fact, it should be, in an escape of this sort, and the practical ingenuity of the trick is something that will not be noticed.

The tank is unprepared; the trick lies in the trunk, which is nothing more nor less than an escape trunk of the well-known style, operating by means of a secret panel in the end, the panel opening inward. A trunk of this type will stand close examination by any committee, and the trunk used in this particular escape, being water-tight and heavy, is particularly well designed to preserve its secret. In the trunk are two flat metal weights. They may be placed in the trunk beforehand, or they may be inserted just before the performer enters. In either event their purpose is too obvious to excite comment. Without them the trunk would not sink; when they are inside the trunk there is no possibility of their removal while the trunk is under water. The weights are in the bottom of the trunk, rather close to the ends, held in place by hooks or fasteners. On the bottom of the tank are two bars or rollers on which the trunk rests. The apparent purpose of these bars, which are rather close together, is to keep the trunk above the bottom of the tank, so that there is no possibility of exit in that direction, and the audience may see under the trunk when it is submerged.

But the weights and the bars serve a much more important purpose than the spectators suppose. Houdini's method would be to remove the weight, when he was in the trunk, from the end where the secret door was situated, and to transfer it to the other end of the trunk, at the same time moving his body to the end with the weights. The bars in the bottom of the tank, being high, crosswise, and close together, would immediately produce the desired result. The heavy end of the trunk would tip so that the trunk would stand on end, the upper end coming just above the level of the water in the tank! The next step would be for Houdini to open the secret panel and make his escape from the trunk, swinging his body over the edge of the tank and bringing the loose weight along with him. By this system he could replace the loose weight in its proper position at the upper end of the trunk, close the secret opening, and give the upper end of the trunk a push that would immediately cause it to drop back and resume its original position.

In a sketch accompanying the explanation of this

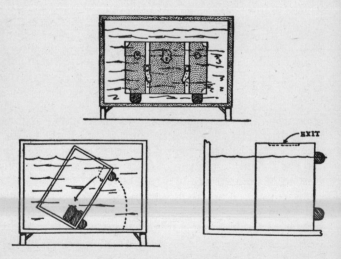

CHANGE OF POSITION IN
THE SUBMERGED TRUNK ENABLING PERFORMER
TO ESCAPE CLEAR OF THE WATER

mystery, Houdini indicated that the cross rods should be attached to the bottom of the trunk and not to the tank itself. This was evidently intended to make the return journey of the trunk a positive matter, the bars having a curved bottom to make the tipping easy. This appears to be the final design of the apparatus. The size and depth of the tank are, of course, important. It must be long to allow for the space into which the trunk turns when on end; it must be deep enough to be convincing, yet shallow enough so that the end of the trunk will emerge. Distance from front to back was reduced to a minimum, so that the rear edge of the tank would be within the performer's reach. The use of very heavy weights is justifiable and logical, for the trunk is supposed to be definitely submerged with no chance of floating. Hence the very factors that aid the performer in his escape are accepted by the spectators as obstacles to his success.

Houdini's notes also mention a canvas cover for the trunk, of the type used in the regular trunk escape. This, of course, is arranged so that the two pieces of canvas may be spread apart above the secret panel. This would necessitate a slight delay, particularly because the canvas would be wet, and Houdini was doubtful whether it would add to the effectiveness of the mystery.

Inasmuch as the usual trunk escape has never lost its popularity, the use of the tank and the submerged trunk, with the mystery of the performer's escaping dry, affords great possibilities for sensational showmanship.

HOUDINI'S DOUBLE BOX MYSTERY

The notes on this escape are dated Berlin, October 29, 1912, 4 A.M. They are written in ink and illustrated with rough diagrams, and it is probable that Houdini had been working since midnight, planning the details of the proposed escape. The notes contain a variety of ideas, and from these a clear impression is gained of the escape as Houdini intended it and of the basic method by which he expected to accomplish it. Some of the mechanical details offer complications, but they do not appear impossible of solution, and the escape is so ingenious and unusual both in effect and method that it offers unusual possibilities. The double box mystery was planned some three years after the submerged trunk escape, and the two escapes are similar in effect, yet entirely different in method of operation. It was Houdini's plan to construct two boxes, one considerably larger than the other, each having a firmly fitting top, particularly the smaller box, which needed to be water-tight. The larger box used in the escape is mounted on heavy legs; the smaller box is similarly mounted and is within the large box, its legs being bolted firmly to the bottom of the large box. The large box has a glass front so that the audience can see the smaller box within.

The performer enters the smaller box; it is locked with a hasp over a staple, and the outer box is flooded with water. As Houdini states in his notes: "The small box is filled with me and air; the large box is filled with water, so that I am completely surrounded by water." There is no necessity for weights on the small box; the legs hold it to the bottom of the large box.

After the large box is locked, the cabinet is placed over the affair, and the performer makes his escape, dry. Yet when the curtains are raised the small box is still fast to the bottom of the large one, locked as it was before the escape.

There are two problems here: the performer must open the boxes, and he must not get wet. The only way of doing this, Houdini decided, is to bring up the small box and open both boxes together. Accordingly he planned to have the boxes act with a very simple and sure release, for he knew that the real mystery centered in the dry escape. "The covers of both boxes," the notes state, "work on the hasps. When the hasp of either box is lowered, it releases all catches, and when I lift up the cover of the small box, I raise it until it lifts up the cover of the large box also."

This was Houdini's original plan; he follows with another arrangement. Figuring that the self-releasing cover would not prove air-tight, he states: "The small box must be air-tight; so the cover must have a round center, on the style of a ship's porthole, so I can unscrew it from the inside.

"The hinges of the large box can be faked so when closed it may be pulled away from the pin hinge by a strong push from beneath, the lock and hasps acting as a hinge."

To make these methods work, the top of the small box must be up against the top of the large box. Unless that is accomplished, it does not matter how the covers are worked. Therefore the crux of the trick is Houdini's method of bringing up the small box. This he proposed to do by having hollow metal legs supporting the small

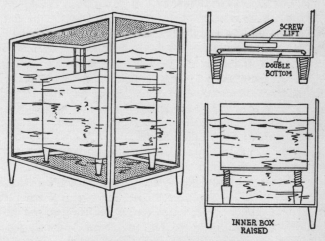

OPERATION OF LIFTING DEVICE IN
THE DOUBLE BOX MYSTERY, SHOWING SMALLER BOX
ABOVE THE SURFACE OF THE WATER

box, each leg to contain a metal screw device, the four operating together under the control of a wrench in the center of the box. Such a box would naturally require a double bottom, with a small compartment between, and a trap or hidden opening which could be lifted to operate the wrench.

Using such a method, the performer proceeds as follows: first he lifts the bottom of the small box and turns the wrench, thus elongating the legs to nearly twice their original height. This brings the top of the small box against the top of the large box. He clamps the wrench in place and raises the covers of both boxes, or opens the porthole in the small box and lifts the cover of the large box. Now, free, he steps from the inner box over the side of the outer one and uses some simple method (such as a chain or a bar) to hold up the small box, while he releases the wrench and replaces the top securely on the small box. The screws are so devised that when the small box is released it will return to its original position. Then the cover is replaced on the large box and fastened there.

Houdini also suggests a porthole in the top of the large box. The object of the porthole in either the small box or in both boxes is to enable members of the committee to see the performer when he is under water. Naturally no suspicion is attached to the porthole in the small box, because it is under water and therefore of no value (presumably) to the performer. The fact that the porthole must be unscrewed from within and later secured from without indicates the use of long and short screws. The long screws are on the inside and hold the porthole firmly in place; the short screws are nothing more than heads tightly inserted from above so that when the inner screws are removed the porthole will be free. In closing the box, the short screws are inserted on the inside of the porthole; the long screws are inserted from the outside, and the device is quite as secure as in the beginning.

This is an escape of the most mysterious type. The

mechanical arrangement of the legs of the smaller box is something which offers considerable difficulty in construction. The lifting of the inner box may not be practical as described, with the simultaneous operation and automatic lowering of the screw devices. Houdini's notes were not the description of a finished piece of apparatus, but were merely preliminary ideas on a new mystery. There are, however, many possibilities for changes and modifications in design, and it is probable that Houdini had in mind the practical plans of construction that would be required.

MILK CAN ESCAPES

The escape from a milk can was performed by Houdini on many occasions. It was an escape that held its popularity and was highly effective; for when Houdini did it, the can was filled with water to make the escape more difficult. Houdini's notes do not contain finished diagrams of special milk cans. There are references to "the old style can," the "1908 can," etc., and these prove that Houdini used several types of milk cans.

In his notes Houdini gives rough sketches that show in part the construction of milk cans, but all these notes refer to improvements or new developments of the trick; therefore the working of the milk can is merely mentioned in passing. Before explaining the working of this device, we must consider the trick as it appears to the audience; for then it will be possible to understand the various additions that Houdini introduced or planned.

The performer exhibits a large milk can. It is a cylinder of metal on which a collar is riveted, and a tapering tube goes up from the collar. A smaller cylinder, or neck, is attached to the tapering tube, and this is provided with staples. The can is filled with water, and the performer enters the can. He is attired in a bathing suit, and he displaces a quantity of water which splashes over the sides of the can and pours itself on a canvas carpet. The cover is a flat lid which is fitted with hasps; it is placed on the milk can, and the hasps are locked to the staples with padlocks. The performer must make his escape in very quick time.

It is understood, of course, that the milk can will bear a close examination. Its simple construction and the fact that it is made entirely of metal make it appear very secure and free from trickery. The simple method of escape depends on the fact that the collar of the tapering portion is not riveted to the top of the large cylindrical portion of the can. The rivets are there, but they are shams. Inside the milk can, the performer can separate the two portions at the joint. This is very practical, and despite its simplicity, it cannot be detected. The secret is safe because the collar fits tightly to the cylinder. It cannot be pulled from its position; no one can obtain a good hold on it. The sides of the collar are slippery (they may even be slightly greased), and there is no possibility of any one's budging it.

But from within the can, the performer is in an ideal position to work. With ordinary effort he can break the neck away from the cylinder and thus escape. The stronger the performer, the easier the escape. By removing the loose section and slinging it out of the way, all difficulties are overcome; and after the escape it is necessary merely to replace the loose portion and make sure that it is firmly in position so that it will again stand inspection.

The bottom of the milk can, riveted in place by an iron band, is a solid article. The band there is exactly like the one at the top, where the can separates. It is very important that the bottom should be tightly joined and well constructed so that there will be no leakage. This is not always possible with the joint at the top. The can is actually loose there, and despite the fact that it cannot be removed from the outside because it fits so tightly, leakage may result. But the can is not entirely filled with water—no water fills the neck; for when the performer enters, there will be an overflow even though the can is only partly filled. Hence nothing betrays the secret before the entry; the can appears quite water-tight in every respect. When the performer goes in, water comes up through the neck and down over the sides of the can; its presence accounts for any water trickling down the sides. The cover is quickly locked, and the escape is under way in the cabinet before any alert committee-man can even begin to make a test for leakage. Hence the secret of this milk can is protected from beginning to end, and it forms a most sensational escape. At the same time, a well-made, tightly fitting can will not leak if the parts are closely joined; this is proven by the double milk can escape, which is explained later.

Among Houdini's notes appears a method of using an *unprepared milk can* which could be used as the genuine commercial article. There are three hasps, solidly attached to the lid of the milk can. The staples are held by single rivets; each rivet comes through from the in side, and is square-bolted on the outside. These rivets are made of brass or copper. When they are put through the neck of the can, felt washers are used so that the heads do not press too tightly against the neck of the can. Everything is genuine, but if these rivets are cut from within, they can be pushed through from the inside and the staples will be free.

To make this method practical, Houdini suggested additional features in his notes. The milk can was to be large, so that there would be space to move freely while at work. The staples should be well down on the neck of the can—possibly attached to the collar below the neck, so as to be quickly and easily reached. The lid of the can was to be raised or bulging upward so that air could be obtained if the work took longer than expected, and the cover was to fit high and have the hasps so placed that the removal of a single staple would enable the performer to open the lid, using the other hasps as hinges. Finally the pliers or nippers were to be provided with a bag-like arrangement so that when the rivet was cut it would drop into the little bag and stay there. In this way the clue of a shining rivet head at the bottom of the milk can would be eliminated.

The notes state: "Have the can made in exact imitation of the can now in use, to deceive them," which shows that Houdini intended to use the unprepared milk can on special occasions. A milk can of this type would prove excellent for lobby display, and would also stand inspection from all points. A person placed inside it would be unable to escape; hence the performer could advertise it heavily. It is one of those escapes which Houdini would not have hesitated to attempt, but the average escape artist would not undertake it, even though he knew the secret and had the appliances.

Working under water when a quick escape was necessary was one of Houdini's accomplishments. He was able to cope with unexpected situations and to overcome obstacles that might—and sometimes did—prove disastrous to his imitators. While this escape is referred to as an "unprepared milk can escape," it depends on a special type of milk can designed for the use of the performer, not self-operating, but vulnerable, from the inside. Houdini's notes go still further with this type of escape and deal with a milk can that may be supplied by any one and that may be specially constructed with the definite purpose of keeping the performer in despite all his efforts.

Houdini's method for an escape from an unprepared milk can *on challenge* depends on the concealment of an assistant in the cabinet which hides the escape. The suggested method of concealment is given in the descriptions of Houdini's cabinet plans. Still the escape is not made certain merely by an assistant's being at hand. Houdini refers to important considerations that should not be neglected, and his idea on the construction of the unprepared can are interesting.

They provide certain factors which are desirable, and

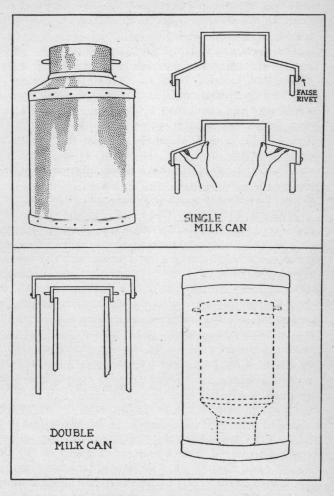

FALSE RIVET

SINGLE
MILK CAN

DOUBLE
MILK CAN

DETAILS OF MILK CAN ESCAPES

which could be incorporated in the construction of the can if made by the performer or if built in accordance with his specifications. Houdini's plans were to make the milk can appear absolutely invulnerable, so that every one would be convinced of its genuineness and it could be examined and left on display indefinitely.

One of his ideas was the use of a glass can. He states: "The top must be made so that it will fit on the outside of the body of the can so that I can breathe until the confederate unlocks or releases the top. Air can enter above the neck, whereas if the lid fits inside, it will make it air-tight. The top must not rest tightly; there must be space for air to circulate.

"A good method of locking the can would be to have heavy steel straps incasing it like a network and have it made so that only one lock has to be opened; also have it fixed so that in case all are 'strange' locks, one rivet can be cut or one nut removed from a bolt, thus allowing the cover to be lifted or shifted. Or arrange it so that only one lock with a special hasp will lock the strap together."

In his notebook Houdini mentions a glass milk can, but suggests one made of metal, as follows: "Have the can made of seamless material or of spun brass. This will show that it is positively impossible for any preparation; the cover or lid can be arranged to lock with one to six locks. The best way is to have the cover fixed permanently with a very heavy hinge so that only one lock will be required. . . .

"In the first method I write that I could use a seamless or spun brass can; this may lead to the thought that there is no preparation and might lead to the fact that I am helped out.

"It would be best to have a suspicious-looking can made. This will attract attention and make them all look for a fake in the can. It is almost imperative that the bell-shaped top be used, so that in case of danger I could have time to get a change of breath, the hollow just allowing that with ease and comfort."

The following notes on the *regular milk can* were typed on a page of Houdini's stationery; they evidently served as memoranda when making plans for the construction of a new milk can. They are not dated, but they are included here because they are typical of many of the original notations that served as references in the preparation of this book:

"Improvements for can.

"Have one made larger. The circle must be at least 17 inches——

"IMPORTANT. Must have a slot or groove to have 'gag' fit at once and no moving, etc. etc.

"Have the top made so that it has a larger lip, and that when it is filled the water must not run over. This is important. Even if we have to put cork or rubber on top of the ledge.

"Handles must be down lower so no cuffs can be hung on to keep the lid on.

"Have all the rivets run in one straight line, and not three like the one now used.

"Have it made air-tight right from the start!!!!!"

THE DOUBLE MILK CAN

The greatest improvement that Houdini contemplated for the milk can escape was the use of two milk cans, one inside the other. This is described in his notebook and is also mentioned in separate notes. Under the heading "Two in One Can Trick," dated Chicago, 1908, Houdini planned to set the regular milk can into a larger can that resembled an ash can and fastened with hasps and staples at the bottom instead of at the top. This is nothing more than the regular milk can trick, using an outer can with the top secretly removable; the top is merely a disc riveted to a heavy collar which clamps down on the cylindrical outer can and gives the appearance of solidity. But in a later development of the escape, Houdini planned to turn the milk can in which he was confined so that it would be upside down when inserted in a larger cylindrical can. The outer can would be filled with water like the inner, yet he would effect his escape.

The notes state: "The trick is to have two cans, one to fit inside of the other. These cans must be large, so that I can stand in them in an upright position and make use of my shoulders in utilizing my strength.

"I am to be placed in one can in a standing position; this is to be turned upside down into the larger can, which is also filled with water. Both cans are locked.

"If the can works on the old style it is best to have the one I get into resting on a bridge or hanging apparatus so the weight of the water will not expose the trick. [This is because the collar that can be pushed upward is fastened to the bottom of the can, the top being genuinely riveted. The bottom will be at the top when the milk can is inverted.]

"The can must be made so that I can turn around and when I am apparently upside down I am turning around and my head and shoulders are up, ready to force the gag so as to get out.

"This wants to be very carefully worked out. The inside can must work at the bottom; the outside can must work at the top, so that both work together and in the same position. If required, the inner can may have a curved top so I can breathe until it is placed into the larger can. This will make the punishment less than if I have to go without breath the entire trick.

"Water can be poured in the outer can so that when the smaller can is placed in the larger can it will splash all over and will be air-tight.

"The inside can cover must be made so that water will not come out when the can is turned over."

In loose notes on this escape, Houdini specifies certain things that must be guarded against. First the inner can must have handles so that it can be put into the larger can. He arranges for such handles on the collar at the bottom. As a result, carrying the can in an up-right position will hold the false bottom in place. The handles are properly situated to appear natural, be-cause the milk can must be tipped over when it is in-serted upside down in the large cylindrical can.

"The cover of the outside can," Houdini stated in his notes, "must be high so that water does not really fill it. This is necessary to allow an air space; and the inner fake can be raised a few inches before touching the outside can, so that I do not have to separate both cans at the same time."

The result is obvious. The performer removes the fake bottom from the inner can almost as soon as the cover of the outer can is in position. He gains air im-mediately. Then he slides the inner can cover aside (allowing time for the cabinet to be placed over the apparatus), and with only the resistance of one cover remaining, the whole affair comes off. A sketch of the outer can shows that the fake lies in the metal collar to which the cover is attached by hasps, the staples being on the collar. Hence it is very similar to the simple method used in the regular milk can escape. From the notes it is evident that Houdini's thought was to create the impression that he could not turn over inside the inner can. With this belief in the minds of the audience, the effectiveness of the escape becomes tremendous.

Part Six

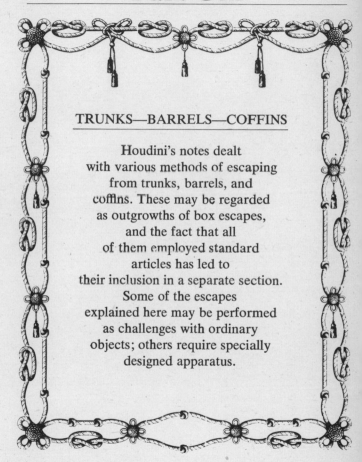

TRUNKS—BARRELS—COFFINS

Houdini's notes dealt
with various methods of escaping
from trunks, barrels, and
coffins. These may be regarded
as outgrowths of box escapes,
and the fact that all
of them employed standard
articles has led to
their inclusion in a separate section.
Some of the escapes
explained here may be performed
as challenges with ordinary
objects; others require specially
designed apparatus.

TRUNK ESCAPES

An escape from an unprepared trunk is not difficult, for the lock of such a trunk is usually fastened by a bolt with a nut on the inside. The trunk is made so that people cannot get in it, not so they cannot get out of it. Unless the clasps are fastened also, the performer who attempts this escape has merely to take off the nut and push out the bolt. A few tools and a flash light are all that are required. With the clasps fastened, the usual procedure is to unscrew the hinges, which are naturally on the inside of the trunk; then the lid can be lifted in reverse fashion.

It is interesting to note that the clasps, which are merely used to prevent strain on the lock and to hold down the ends of the cover, become a real barrier when the trunk is used as an object in which to confine a person. Houdini, however, had methods of overcoming them. He mentions these in his description of a rawhide trunk to be used as a challenge. The locks on the rawhide trunk could be made so that no bolt and nut arrangement would be usable. With such a trunk, Houdini planned special locks that could be unlocked from the inside, probably with a small key, or through a tiny hole in the lock which could be managed with a pin.

The first method of pushing back the clasps is to use a thin awl-like instrument; this is particularly adapted to the rawhide trunk, as the trunk itself could be pierced. The other method, which is possible with various types of trunks, is quite simple. The performer puts his head against the top of the trunk and presses upward; then he strikes the front of the trunk with his fist, hitting directly in back of the clasp. A well-directed blow will knock the clasp loose.

Houdini mentions a tin trunk fitted with a lock operating from the inside as well as from the outside, yet able to stand examination. It was used by a performer called Hanco, who escaped from the trunk while under water, by the simple method of opening the cover. While performing in an Australian town, Hanco unlocked the trunk too soon; and as it happened to turn while it was being let down from a bridge, the performer fell out before he reached the water, much to the amusement of the crowd.

An ingenious idea in connection with trunk escapes appears in Houdini's notes. It is specially applicable to an unprepared trunk. Some trunks have linings of cloth, and this must be cut to enable the performer to get at the lock or the hinges. To render the escape effective, the escape artist must repair the damage, unless he does not permit an examination after the trick is over. This work is not difficult; a supply of duplicate cloth and a bottle of glue will suffice. But Houdini developed this idea to the extent of having a solidly lined trunk which appeared to have an interior made of wood that was not removable. Instead of using wood, he planned to use heavy paper which resembled wood; this material would appear formidable; yet it would be no barrier to the performer. By tearing the paper away he could get at the parts of the trunk where operation was necessary, and after the escape he could reline the trunk with whatever amount of paper was needed, utilizing a supply hidden in the cabinet.

There are various forms of trunks designed for escape work. There is a similarity between them and certain types of boxes which have hinged covers. Houdini refers to various types of trunks and boxes in his notes and includes a brief description of a trunk-like box lined with zinc that can be filled with water while the performer is inside. This device was designed to work at the hinges, which had special removable pins. The essential difference between a box escape and a trunk escape is that the former involves a roughly made article which is nailed at the top, while the latter requires a permanently constructed device which is used indefinitely, locks, bolts, or clasps being used to fasten the outside.

The famous box trick performed by Maskelyne in England many years ago was really the original trunk trick. A reward of £500 was offered to any one who could duplicate the mystery, and it was won by Dr. J. W. Lynn in 1898. Dr. Lynn's box had an entire panel that was removable; it slid up and down between the framework at the top and bottom of the box. It was held up by a small marble located in a groove directly under the panel and also by a concealed spring. After the performer was locked in the box and a canvas cover placed on it, assistants moved the box to show all sides, and the tipping process caused the marble to roll to the end of the groove and into a shorter groove that ran along the front of the box at the bottom. By inserting his fingers in air-holes, the performer was able to pull the panel downward and inward and then untie or loosen the cord holding the canvas cover. When this box was right side up, with the marble in position, its secret was absolutely undetectable, for the panel could not be opened. When the box was placed on end, the panel worked automatically.

BARREL AND CASK ESCAPES

One of the most convincing escapes described by Houdini is that from a large barrel or cask. The simplicity of the article impresses the audience. No locks or attachments are necessary. When the performer is placed inside and the barrel is headed, escape certainly seems to be impossible. Houdini's notes describe several methods of escaping from a barrel. This trick was done as a challenge, and from one set of instructions it is evident that Houdini used it himself. In the construction of an ordinary barrel, the staves are provided with grooves at the inner ends. The bottom is fitted into the grooves and the band is driven on, holding the staves together. The same process is applied to the top. With tight-fitting ends and metal hoops around the sides a strong barrel or cask cannot be broken open from the inside. Yet in this escape, the performer must manage to open the barrel and later show it in its original condition.

For *the barrel challenge* the performer uses a barrel which may be provided by the challengers. It must, of course, be large enough to contain him comfortably. This challenge was usually accepted by a brewery; when delivered, the bottom of the barrel was already in place. All that remained was to insert the top and drive the upper band firmly into place. This system makes the actual imprisonment the work of a very few minutes; the escape from an ordinary barrel requires a much longer time.

Houdini's instructions follow: "My original method was to have the top of the barrel made in several sections, with plenty of air-holes. The middle board should have at least five or six (the more the better) in a cross-row.

"I would take one dozen fine key-hole saws and a strong handle with me in the barrel, having previously obtained duplicate boards from the brewery.

"Inside the barrel, I would fasten two stage screws in the top and then start cutting with the saws, to cut the board in half.

"After cutting the board, I would be able to give a few hard pulls (using the stage screws) and thus draw the sections of the board inside the barrel.

"You can use two rows of holes so that in case the board is in too tight, you can cut both lines of holes, thereby taking out a piece of the board, making the rest short enough to draw out, no matter how tightly it may have been placed in."

The removal of the center board makes it possible to draw the other boards toward the center, where the distance is greater than at the sides; thus these boards are drawn in intact. The performer is provided with duplicates of all the boards, concealed in the cabinet, in case it proves necessary to saw one of the smaller boards.

The instructions continue: "After making your escape, dig up the duplicate middle board, take a muffled hammer (any hammer which you have padded beforehand), and knock up the hoops. This is easy after you have taken the top out. Replace the boards and drive down the hoops.

"Before entering the barrel make a speech stating that you are not certain of escaping and that you will try for at least an hour before giving up. You should be able to do the job in thirty minutes.

"After starting the cutting with the keyhole saw it is a good plan to have a small fine hardwood saw also; this will cut more quickly.

"Be sure and try this escape before you go after it. Also take along a couple of electric pocket lamps; they will come in handy, as this 'gag' will take an awful lot of work."

In another set of instructions on the barrel challenge, Houdini suggests that the bottom be made of several pieces (presumably so that the top may be a solid piece of wood). In this case the performer must saw on the bottom, cutting it and removing; it may be replaced by a board of pliable wood, which can be forced into place, especially if slightly shortened. The smaller boards go back in the same way they came out—by sliding from the center to the sides. This requires air-holes in the bottom; whichever is used, top or bottom, it is important that the air-holes should be placed exactly the same as in the original board. This indicates that they are made when the barrel is constructed. If the committee should make the air-holes just before the performance, the performer would require a brace and bit among the items hidden in the cabinet.

Inasmuch as barrels differ, the performer who ac-

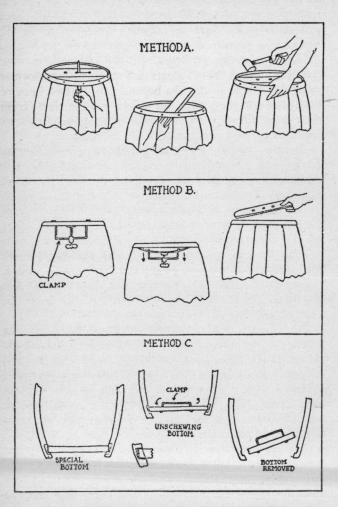

EXPLANATORY DIAGRAMS OF BARREL ESCAPES

cepts this challenge must make arrangements according to the circumstances. If the top is formed of several narrow strips, it will be necessary to cut two of them instead of one. Cleats or wooden cross-braces on the top can be permitted; these are screwed to the boards that form the top, and they add to the length of time required. When outer cleats are used, the performer must cut a hole in the top board, through two lines of air-holes, and thus reach out to unscrew the cleats from the center board. With the center board gone, the other screws are easily reached from within the barrel.

Another method given by Houdini requires that the center board in the top be made of pliable wood. The air-holes are in the side sections, of which there are two, and the performer has a strong wrench or screw device specially designed for the trick. Two clamps project from this, and the ends turn at an angle. They are adjustable and are fitted into air-holes in the side boards, hooking on the outside. The performer turns the screw and it presses against the center board, gradually bending it upward in the middle until it is finally forced free. This board must have no air-holes, or it may break.

Having stepped out of the barrel, the performer bends the board and forces it back into the top of the barrel, using the wrench for this purpose. This method is specially suited to large-headed casks, and possesses the advantage of requiring no duplicate boards. It probably requires a great deal of effort, but if conditions are suitable for it, it should save time and reduce the number of operations required.

The *false-bottomed barrel* requires preparation and hence is not suitable for a challenge. It is a very ingenious idea, inasmuch as the bottom may be fitted to a thick barrel of the proper size and everything may be examined before and after the trick. The top of the barrel is put on by the committee. The bottom of this barrel consists of two parts, one a wooden hoop threaded on the inside, the other a wooden disc threaded on the outer edge. The solid portion screws into the hoop, which is fitted in the barrel. Theoretically the hoop should fit in the barrel so that although the hoop tapers slightly on the outside the interior is straight, and when the false bottom is screwed in the joint will be close enough to the barrel staves to be undetectable.

From the outside of the barrel the join cannot possibly be observed. The inside of the bottom cannot be so closely inspected, because of the depth of the barrel. The sides must be very thick in order to contain the wooden hoop, for the hoop cannot be too flimsy. The false bottom cannot be unscrewed by the hands alone, which makes its secret doubly safe. The performer does the work with the aid of a piece of apparatus shaped somewhat like the handle of a flat-iron. He pushes the projecting arms into convenient air-holes and thus gains sufficient leverage to unscrew the false bottom, which is made from a single piece of wood. He can then turn the bottom edgeways inside the barrel and make his escape. Fitting the false bottom back into position, he can again tighten it with the special apparatus. This escape would require a large cask, allowing plenty of space inside; and it appears that the barrel should be placed on its side in a trestle or turned upside down, as it would otherwise be difficult for the performer to find a suitable place to rest while unscrewing the false bottom.

The *side-trap barrel* is covered in some brief notes. This is another type of specially constructed barrel, having an opening on one side near the bottom. This type of barrel is not intended for very close inspection; it seems to have been designed more for an illusion involving the disappearance of a girl than for escape purposes, although it could be used as an escape. The barrel staves are incomplete on one side; they run two thirds of the distance down and end at a broad hoop. The remaining section is formed by short staves fastened together; these can be removed and replaced; they form a secret trap. Inner hoops should be used on this barrel so that the join of the sections will not be noticed. The lower end of the trap is evidently fitted into the bottom of the barrel; by pushing up the inner hoop, the trap may be removed. When the performer is out, the inner hoop is pulled down and the outer hoop is slightly raised, allowing the proper insertion of the trap, after which the outer hoop is pushed back in place. Well designed, a barrel of this type would appear quite unprepared and would be capable of standing an ordinary examination.

The *double barrel* was not used by Houdini; it was designed by another performer as an under-water escape. Houdini pasted an account of the trick in his notebook and eventually learned the secret, which he added in a brief notation. The barrel was specially designed to come apart. It evidently had hoops inside and out, to cover the break. The two portions were held together by bayonet catches that the performer could release when inside the barrel. By turning the top portion in the proper way, the barrel separated immediately.

This type of barrel was not intended for the stage, but it would evidently have served such a purpose in the average escape act. As a release, it was well suited to a quick escape while under water, for by a simple operation at the desired moment the performer was able to free himself without difficulty and thus be clear before his lungs required air. The top of the barrel was headed in the usual manner. During this delay the man inside had time to free himself from handcuffs and shackles that had been placed on his arms and legs. The bottom of the barrel was loaded with pig iron, and the sides were drilled with holes so that the barrel would sink rapidly. As the performer was unable to put the barrel together while under water, he was forced to leave it at the bottom of the river. A rope was attached so that the barrel could be retrieved some time after the escape.

THE GREAT COFFIN IMPOSTURE

This trick was exposed by Houdini in England on September 30, 1904, and an account of the exposé appeared in a London newspaper the following day. The trick had been advertised in England as an escape from a genuine unprepared coffin by one of Houdini's imitators, and Houdini proved that these claims were false. The coffin used in the trick was a wooden one, put on display before performances. It was brought on the stage a short while before the act, and the performer who exhibited it took his position in the coffin and allowed members of the committee to screw the lid down tight. He took longer than half an hour for the escape and reappeared before the audience in a semiconscious condition, as though completely exhausted by a terrific struggle. Houdini stated that the claims regarding the coffin escape were misrepresentations and that the long time required by the performer was purely humbug. Hence he demonstrated that the trick could be accomplished in less than one minute and that the coffin was prepared before the performance. When Houdini exhibited the trick, he proved these statements. He also offered a large reward to any one who could escape from the coffin without resorting to the preparation. The performer who had advertised the trick did not appear to collect.

The method used in the coffin imposture was quite simple. The coffin could be left in the lobby of the theater up to a short time before it was required, as the preparation was a matter of a very few minutes. The wooden pieces of the coffin were held together by screws on the outside. The lid was actually held down by clamps and could not be opened by the man inside. The head panel, however, was a short piece fitted in between the sides. It was held in place by three-inch screws that extended through the sides, close to the ends. Without these screws, the panel could be removed with ease.

In his exposé of the coffin trick, Houdini simply removed the three-inch screws and replaced them with one-inch screws. The coffin had been open for inspection prior to this; the faking was done when the coffin was off-stage, and the committee was satisfied that the coffin had not been exchanged for another. The cursory examination did not discover the loose head panel. Inside the coffin, Houdini removed the panel, took out the short screws, and put the panel back in place, fastening it there with the three-inch screws that had originally been in the coffin. This was the regular method used by the imitator who introduced the coffin trick; after each escape the coffin was thoroughly examined, then placed in the theater lobby until a short time before the next exhibition.

SHEET IRON COFFIN ESCAPE

Houdini describes for this trick a metal coffin which may be made of brass or sheet iron. He wrote the explanation and diagrams on August 10, 1910, while aboard the S.S. *Mauretania*. There have been various escapes from coffin-shaped boxes; this one is based on a novel adaptation of an older principle. The sides, ends, and bottom of the coffin are riveted together, giving a very solid appearance. The top is broken in the center and forms two covers, one opening on hinges toward the head, the other toward the feet.

The performer is placed in the coffin and the lids are lowered. The top and upper edges of the sides have metal flanges, drilled with holes. Bolts and nuts or padlocks are used to fasten these flanges together, so that there is absolutely no possibility of the top's being lifted. As a final assurance, there are bolts on one lid and sockets on the other; these are joined, and the top of the coffin forms as solid a barrier as the bottom. Yet the escape artist can make his exit in less than one minute. This coffin was designed to stand inspection, open and closed, before and after the trick. Furthermore, it is one test in which the performer requires no concealed appliances to aid him in the escape. When the coffin is opened, committee-men may climb in it and test it as much as they please. When it is closed and locked they can try to open it either before or after the performer has made his escape; yet they will have no results, even if they look in the right place for the escape. For there is only one way to operate it; that is from the inside when the coffin is closed, and the performer is the only person who has that opportunity.

The head end of the coffin is loose. The rivets that apparently hold it to the sides are faked and do not enter the end. The end fits very tight, however, so that it is firmly in place and appears to be a solid part of the coffin. When the upper half of the lid is opened, the end acts as a solid piece, the hinges serving the lid. But when the lid is closed and locked down, the conditions are reversed. The hinges now serve for the end, which swings outward when pressed from within.

Houdini's explanatory notes show clearly the principle on which this device operates; they do not, however, include certain details of construction which are necessary. If the end is merely held in by pressure, or by close fitting, close examination such as striking the end is not advisable while the coffin is opened. At that time, the false end must support the weight of the opened lid. A square-posted framework for the interior of the coffin is a natural item of construction, and this will prevent the end from swinging inward when the cover is swung back. When the lid is opened to its full extent, the position of the hinges makes it impossible to swing the end outward. It can only be pushed when the cover is closed. With the cover closed the end cannot be opened from the outside, for it is tightly fitted and there is no projection that will serve as a hold for pulling the end. In brief, the false end operates only from the inside when the lids are shut.

The notes specify that the coffin should be of sufficient size for Houdini to turn over inside it. He planned to lie on his back when entering the coffin, and to turn on to his stomach after the casket was locked. This indicates that the end would be tightly fitted or fastened from the inside; otherwise backward pressure of the hands would be sufficient and there would be no necessity for the performer's changing his position. The fact that the head end and not the foot end was chosen for the fake gives the same indication. Pressure with the feet would be more effective; therefore the use of the hands shows clearly that some mechanical operation was considered.

Special rivets or metal screws attaching the end section to the inside framework of the coffin would hold the end secure, would pass inspection, and would allow any amount of pressure against the trick end while the coffin was open. These would probably require a tool for their removal or loosening. The fake rivets on the outside of the coffin are the important factor so far as the committee is concerned. Their genuine appearance indicates solidity, and the ingenious method of switching the use of the hinges from the cover to the end is the vital principle of the escape. The other details of construction are minor matters that Houdini evidently intended to add in the finished plans.

THE METAL CASKET ESCAPE

This is an escape from an oval-shaped casket which is made of solid metal, all parts riveted in place. It is heavily constructed and makes a very good showing, as it will stand close examination. The casket is encircled by a strip of band iron. Instead of a flange, the strip is supplied with metal angles which terminate in flat

projections. A similar band is riveted to the bottom
of the cover, which fits over the casket, so that when
the cover is on, the projections of both bands
correspond. The projections are drilled with holes;
these admit bolts or padlocks to fasten the cover securely to the casket.

The performer enters the casket and the cover is
placed on it. The cover is made in two sections, hinging
above the center, so that the top portion may be turned
down to show the performer in position. When the
cover is entirely closed, the members of the committee
fasten the projections alternately with bolts and padlocks; the employment of different types of fastenings is
quite effective. After the casket is placed within the
cabinet the performer makes his escape in a short space
of time, and when the cabinet is removed, the casket is
shown still locked.

The casket is quite as solid as it appears. The secret
of the escape lies in the metal band that encircles it.
This is not part of the casket; the rivets that seem to
hold it are false. The casket is slightly larger at the
bottom than at the top; hence the metal band slides
down to the center and may be pressed firmly into place
at the spot where it is supposed to be riveted. In examining the casket, no member of the committee can discover this false condition, for it is impossible to exert
enough force on the small projections to move the
band. Even with several persons tugging at them at
once, the band is too firm to be raised. Committee-men
seldom act in unison; even if they should, they would
get no results, for the band is very firmly in position.

When the cover is on, the situation remains the
same. The small projections are quite as difficult to
grasp; the weight of the cover adds to the solidity of the
device. But inside the casket, the escape artist possesses
a decided advantage. By raising his back against the
inside of the cover or by using his feet to exert pressure,
he can push the cover upward, and it will take the
metal band of the casket along with it. He does not

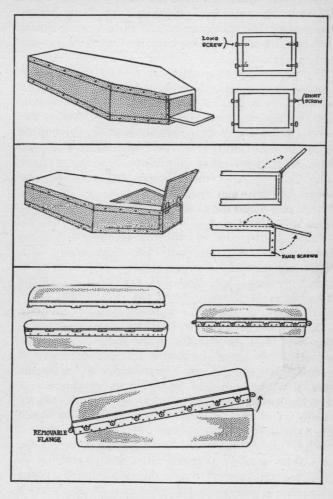

TOP—THE GREAT COFFIN IMPOSTURE
CENTER—THE SHEET IRON COFFIN ESCAPE
BOTTOM—THE METAL CASKET ESCAPE

attempt to lift the entire cover; that would be too difficult because of the weight. Pressure at different spots gradually loosens the iron band, and the performer exerts all his strength at one end. This causes the end of the cover to come up, the other end serving as a support.

As soon as he has raised the cover sufficiently, the escapist slips out through the space that he has provided. Then he carefully lets the end of the coffin back into position and pounds it down so that the iron band is once more firmly attached to the casket. Meanwhile the orchestra obliges with loud music, which effectually drowns any noise that may come from the cabinet. After the escape, everything stands the usual inspection. The casket is locked in identically the same manner as before; when the bolts and padlocks are removed, the cover may be lifted and the opened casket submitted to the same examination as before the escape.

THE GALVANIZED IRON COFFIN

The escape from a coffin made of galvanized iron is explained in unfinished notes which make the idea clear but which end with suggestions of various ways in which the coffin could be constructed. This is because of certain obstacles encountered in the mechanical arrangement; and the interpretation of the notes on this escape was unusually difficult. The coffin is intended to be hexagonal in shape. There are four long, tapering sides and two short ends. At every one of the six corners, there are flat upright posts or braces, both inside and out; also cross-braces at the ends and the center, both inside and outside of the coffin.

The coffin is thus a six-cornered framework into which solid pieces of galvanized iron have been riveted to form the sides and bottom of the coffin. There are eight of these pieces, six for the sides and two for the bottom. The upper edge of the coffin is a wide, flat flange, riveted in place. It extends over the inner portion of the coffin, as well as outward. The cover (which resembles the coffin, but is not so deep) fits on this flange, and it has a similar flange. The outer rims of both flanges are provided with holes for bolts or locks. Altogether it is a most solid-looking device; yet it is designed for a very quick release.

To understand the working of this device we must consider the coffin during its construction. Actually it is nothing but a framework of braces which support the flange. There are no braces at the ends. The cover is not considered, as it is without preparation. Now if this coffin were rectangular instead of hexagonal (a possible construction mentioned in the notes) it would be a simple matter to construct two drawers which would slide in and out between the braces In position, they would appear solid. Braces or framework at the ends would be permissible then, for they would be attached to the end of each drawer—not to the actual framework supporting the wide flange. To escape from this device, the performer would have very little to do. By pushing in opposite directions, the coffin being short, he could push the two portions apart.

The fault of the rectangular construction is that there is no excuse for the center braces which hide the joint of the two sections. The hexagonal construction interferes with the sliding apart of the drawers, because the sides are tapering. This must be overcome in the construction of the coffin. Each end has four side braces that are upright, two inside the coffin and two outside. The two outside braces are not attached to the flange, but to the sides themselves. Hence when the drawerlike portions are pushed apart, they travel with them. It is not necessary for the bottom to go with the sides and ends. It can be permanently attached to the genuine braces that support the flange.

The coffin should not be too long; by extending his hands and pushing one way while his feet push the other, the performer can separate the parts and make his escape. One end of the coffin—that is, one entire half—may be permanently in position, for the performer can simply push the other end open and make his escape quite as easily. The cover rests on the flange throughout the escape and does not figure in the working. All parts are riveted; many of the rivets are false.

The ultimate construction of this device may be analyzed thus: A framework supporting a flat flange, and permitting the insertion of a drawer from each end. All parts are riveted at the end that does not operate. The end that must be removable is so arranged that no framework is attached both to the flange and to the drawer. All parts are attached to the flange, with the exception of those which would interfere with the operation; those are attached to the drawer. False rivets are used wherever genuine ones would make trouble. The double framework at the center covers up the joint; the wide flange extending inward and outward hides the sliding upper edges of the sides. Properly constructed, this coffin is extremely ingenious, and with tight-fitting parts it cannot be operated except from the inside.

Part Seven

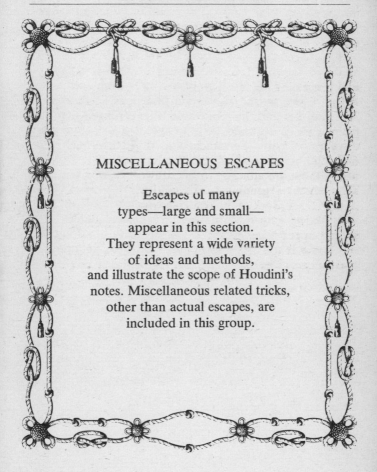

MISCELLANEOUS ESCAPES

Escapes of many
types—large and small—
appear in this section.
They represent a wide variety
of ideas and methods,
and illustrate the scope of Houdini's
notes. Miscellaneous related tricks,
other than actual escapes, are
included in this group.

The escape from a wooden log was an idea planned by Houdini and mentioned in a very short memorandum. The performer was to be bound to a wooden log, with ropes or chains, from which he would escape. In order to accomplish this escape, Houdini planned to have a special log constructed; the log would be cut in two sections and rejoined by a heavy screw. Bound to such a log, the performer, by separating the two portions, could release himself by sliding the ropes or chains to the center. The exact method of binding is not given; it would be planned so that the separation of the log would be possible and would also be of advantage to the performer.

Conceivably the performer might be held by short chains encircling the log, the ends of the log set in solid stands and held there by bolts passing through the outer ends of the logs. In brief, the primary object would be to prove that no chain could be slipped over the end of the log. Houdini suggested that the log be made in Germany and evidently intended to give the device further consideration, for his notes were made while aboard the steamer Kaiser Wilhelm II. If the special log could be constructed as Houdini proposed to have it, it would form the important part of a simple but highly effective escape.

PILLORY ESCAPES

Three methods of escaping from a pillory in which the performer's head and hands are imprisoned are explained in Houdini's notes. The earliest reference to this sort of escape is dated Liverpool, October 22, 1904.

A

Pillory Number One is very ingenious. The lower half is mounted on two posts and is made in two sections. Starting with the inside of one post, a cut runs to a wrist-hole, then curves down below the neck-hole, and comes up to the other wrist-hole and down to the inside of the other post. A secret hinge holds it to the post at one end; a catch holds it to the post at the other.

To hide the cut, the posts and lower part of the pillory are decorated with a brass binding which follows the break, just touching the lower edges of the wrist-holes. Fake rivets in the brass binding reënforce the deception. The performer releases himself by kicking the post that has the catch. This releases the catch and the lower section of the pillory breaks apart, allowing ample space for the performer to remove his head and hands. The apparatus is easily restored to its original condition.

B

Pillory Number Two is a very simple yet effective form of release. The lower half of the pillory is mounted on a frame, while the upper section is either loose or hinged, so that when the performer places his wrists and neck on the semicircles in the lower section, the upper half may be closed to imprison him. Then the pillory is locked and the performer is firmly held in position. Yet his escape is very easy. The holes in the pillory are bound with leather so that they can fit tight against the performer's neck and wrists. The leather binding extends up the sides of the pillory. The pillory is faked beneath the leather. The holes are really much larger than they appear, but are fitted with curved blocks to which the leather is attached. All the performer has to do is to draw his head and hands backward and the curved blocks come out, releasing him

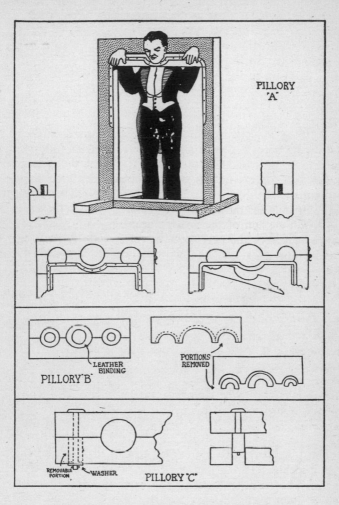

PILLORY 'A'

PILLORY 'B'

LEATHER BINDING

PORTIONS REMOVED

REMOVABLE PORTION — WASHER

PILLORY 'C'

EXPLANATORY DIAGRAMS OF PILLORY ESCAPES

completely. The portions removed from the pillory are
then replaced.

The notes mention a spring to release these parts of
the pillory, but the details are not specified. Some such
mechanical device is necessary to make the pillory really effective and to allow it to pass inspection. The
release can be arranged with the closing of the pillory
or by a spring touched afterward by the performer. The
pillory in the form described is simply an idea that
requires further development.

C

Pillory Number Three is held together by long bolts
which pass through vertical holes in the sections of it.
The bolts are genuine and may be sealed after they are
in position. The lower half of the pillory is affixed to a
stand and the upper portion is set on it. The ends of the
holes through which the bolts pass are strengthened by
large metal washers which are placed in position. These
washers have an outside diameter greater than the
heads of the bolts. The lower part of the pillory has
large plugs through which the bolt-holes are drilled.

The performer is bent well forward when in the pillory; by a straight upward lift he raises the top portion
and the plugs are pulled out of the lower half, so that
he is released. The plugs are held by catches which are
opened by the performer, who presses nails on the sides
or front of the pillory. This mechanical arrangement is
not described in detail, but it could easily be worked
out. The plugs must be carefully and neatly made, so
that they are well concealed in the pillory. They are, of
course, much larger than the bolts, and a trifle larger
than the washers.

THE GLASS CYLINDER

The device used in this escape consists of a cylinder made entirely of heavy glass and a glass cover that fits over the cylinder. There are either four or eight handles or flanges on the cover, which are open in the center. The bottom of the cylinder is solid; everything is made entirely of glass. The sketch shows no air-holes, and it is probable that none were intended, for a reason that will be mentioned later. The performer is placed in the glass cylinder, and the cover is set on it. The edge of the cover extends several inches down on the cylinder, so that the performer is very effectively bottled within. As there are no places for locks, the cylinder is secured with straps. These pass through the openings in the handles on the outside of the cover and are fastened.

The description refers to four straps; this may mean *two* long straps that appear as four when they entirely circle the cylinder, or it may mean four straps that would appear as eight. Two straps seem likeliest. These straps can also be connected by cross-straps, forming a meshwork about the cylinder. The performer makes his escape from the cylinder while it is concealed from view, and after his escape it is still strapped.

The escape depends entirely on the straps; they are ordinary straps that will stand examination, but they are handled to the performer's advantage. When the straps are drawn tight, they bind in passing through the openings on the side of the cover. This makes it impossible to pull them too tight, although they appear tight. The height of the cylinder and the length of the straps aid in this deception. Although the performer is apparently in a tightly sealed device, he can take advantage of the slack in the straps by pushing the cover upward. It takes considerable pushing to draw the straps farther through the openings, but the performer has the ad-

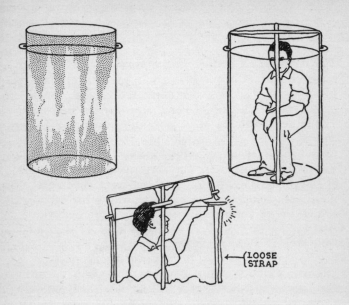

DETAILS OF THE GLASS CYLINDER SHOWING
ACTION OF ESCAPE

vantage of a strong, well-distributed pressure, for he is
centralizing his efforts on the cover and is drawing the
straps straight up, whereas the committee-men were
forced to pull the straps downward from the openings.
That is, the straps are a little too large for the holes, but
they can be worked through. The performer finally
manages to raise the cover sufficiently to slide a knife
between the cover and the cylinder and thus cut the
straps. A flexible knife with a curved blade is helpful. It
is not necessary to cut every strap that appears on the
sides of the cylinder. Two cuts will sever the straps that
appear as four. Then the cover is free and the performer can lift it.

There are several items worth considering: first, a
loose-fitting cover that is helpful when the knife is used;
next, the absence of air-holes. This is an excuse to

hurry the strapping, as it is evident that the performer must hurry and cannot be delayed. Air-holes would also work against the trick because of the possibility of pushing an implement through them to the straps. With the straps buckling on top, the tightness is deceptive and seems much greater than it actually is. The object being to hold the cover firmly, the persons buckling the straps believe that the tightness at the top indicates tightness throughout. The meshwork or connecting straps at the sides also give the appearance, when used, of additional security. They are tight and therefore add to the deception.

Out of the cylinder, the performer can replace the cut straps with genuine ones concealed in the cabinet. If the meshwork is used, this, the notes suggest, might not be necessary, owing to the presence of so many straps. The cut straps could be drawn tightly together and fastened underneath one of the cross-straps, and the performer can dismiss the committee before any one has an opportunity to discover this. A few pushes on the top will convince the committee that the cover is still firmly in position. The cylinder can be made of glass and metal instead of glass alone; so constructed it must be designed to prove clearly that it is unprepared. The simplicity of this escape may create the impression that the method would be obvious. This is extremely doubtful. Straps can be straight without being tight, and they will appear tight. The best tricks are often the simplest—when the secret is known—and this escape possesses features that are favorable to successful presentation.

THE GLASS TUBE TEST

Houdini was ever active, and it appears that ocean voyages, with their periods of enforced inactivity, either stimulated him to new ideas or gave him the opportunity to set down plans that were formulating in his mind. His notes for an escape from a glass tube, like other excellent ideas, was drawn up on board a transatlantic liner. No date appears on these notes; they were made on the S.S. *Mauretania*, probably during the voyage of August, 1910, when he planned a coffin escape.

In many of his notes Houdini describes a piece of apparatus in considerable detail and adds a very brief and somewhat obscure explanation; in the glass tube escape he followed the opposite procedure. The only part that is doubtful is the appearance of the tube itself; the methods of escape—of which there are several— are quite clear. The tube was intended to be made partly of glass and partly of metal, the purpose of the glass being to increase the effectiveness of the trick; for secret traps and springs cannot be used in glass apparatus. The cover of this device is like the porthole of a ship, a piece of glass set in a metal frame; the tube itself was to be of glass, either a single piece in cylindrical form with a metal bottom, a single piece with metal bands at both top and bottom, or a glass cylinder set in a metal framework with long openings in the sides so that the glass would be visible. This would make the sides of the tube invulnerable, and false rivets at the top or sides would be unusable, since the examiners could see them through the glass.

The tube thus designed holds the performer in an upright position, with just sufficient space in which to move. Turning upside down in the tube is impossible. The top is hinged, the hinges held with rivets to the upper portion of the tube. On the other side a staple is fastened to the upper part of the tube, and the top has a hasp attached. This allows a padlock to hold the cover firmly in place. An optional method is a cover fitting over the top of the glass tube; bolts are pushed out from the inside, and the committee-men fasten padlocks to openings in the bolts. Houdini devised five methods of escaping from this contrivance; some of them were adaptations of methods used in other escapes; others were designed for this trick alone. All of them required working at the top.

In the *first method* genuine rivets are used to hold the top to the glass tube. The performer has a plierlike cutter that enables him to cut the rivets, either at the hinge or at the staple. The cut rivets are forced through by the performer, and he is able to open the top of the tube so that he can escape. The lock must then be opened with a duplicate key so that he can replace the cut rivets with others that will stand ordinary examination. He then relocks the cover in position.

The *second method* requires the use of bolts. The bolts first shown are genuine; the performer exchanges them for bolts from which the heads may be unscrewed. This would be difficult to do inside the tube, as the performer would be visible to the persons outside. Houdini evidently intended that the exchange should be made before entering the tube, or else that the bolts should be so well constructed that they would pass the examination of the committee. It is probable that he considered the latter method, since he evidently possessed bolts that would stand inspection.

The *third method* is quite ingenious, and well adapted to this particular trick. The tube is not of great diameter; hence the lock is not far distant from the performer. Its inaccessibility is evident, however, and it seems quite apparent that a standard padlock of strong construction is all that is required to keep the performer from escaping. In this method Houdini depended on large air-holes in the glass top. Through one of these, near the side, he intended that the performer should push an extension key—a key that could open the padlock and that could be operated by the rod that holds it. With such a key, the performer reaches the padlock and unlocks it; then he uses the key to shake the padlock from the staple. It is evident that in this method two staples should be used instead of a hasp fitting over a staple, for lifting the hasp with the extension key would require an additional operation; whereas it would be nearly as easy to lift the padlock from two staples as from one. Thus disposing of the padlock, the performer can raise the top of the tube, make his exit, and replace the padlock. In the *fourth method* all parts on the outside of the tube are inaccessible; the air-holes in the glass are small; all rivets or bolts are genuine and are not attacked or manipulated. The top itself cannot be worked from within the tube; in fact the performer is actually bottled up in a most convincing fashion. To make his escape, the performer requires a special device of screw pattern. He conceals this on his person and has it in the tube. The apparatus consists of a disc just the size of the glass in the top of the tube. This has threaded holes which correspond with certain air-holes in the glass.

The performer pushes several iron rods through the

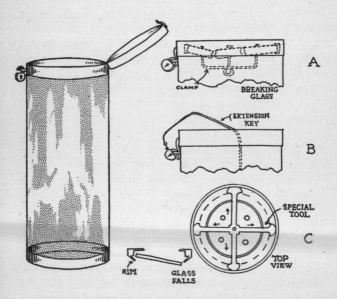

THE ESCAPE TUBE, WITH EXPLANATORY DIAGRAMS
SHOWING THREE METHODS OF ESCAPE

air-holes. These rods have projecting angles; the angle of a rod is inserted first; then the rod is turned so that the performer can reach over the edge of the disc and engage the lower end of the iron in the correct hole in the disc. These rods are arranged with threads for the attachment of little levers or winged clamps. By operating these from below, the performer gradually tightens the disc against the glass, and as he continues pressure, the glass breaks or is crushed. He carefully removes enough glass to reach out and operate the lock. Opening the top of the tube, he makes his escape, takes the cover apart from the outside, and inserts a new piece of glass which has been hidden in the cabinet and which is the exact duplicate of the original glass (i.e. containing air-holes of the same size and in the same position). Then he is able to arrange everything from the outside so that the glass tube and its cover are in their original condition.

It would seem as though the performer could make his escape by removing all the broken glass and passing through the space thus provided; then by removing the top rim he could replace the glass without opening the cover. But Houdini does not mention this in his plans; the assumption therefore is that the rim containing the glass is quite large, and the diameter of the hole is insufficient for the performer to emerge without lifting the cover. This, however, has an advantage over the extension key method, as Houdini provided a way of completing the trick in case the hasp was locked to the staple with a lock that could not be easily opened—a "strange lock," as he terms it. To do this, the hasp is made in two pieces, the top piece bolted to the lower and also to the cover, but entirely outside the top, so that it cannot be handled from within the tube while the glass is there. If the lock cannot be operated, the performer uses a pair of cutters to clip the upper section of the hasp. This enables him to open the top, and he replaces the cut portion of the hasp with a duplicate section.

The *fifth method* is quite as ingenious as the fourth; the removal of the glass is also essential, but the glass is not broken. The glass does not go deep into the metal rim that supports it; yet it cannot be removed without the aid of a special implement. The performer has an instrument with four flat arms, each terminating in a head with curved edge. These enter a center block which is provided with a screw to force the arms outward. The performer sets this against the glass and turns the screw to force the arms toward the sides. The edges are knife-like, and the glass is forced upward a fraction of an inch so that the heads of the instrument enter between the metal and the glass. The metal rim is not thick, and as the performer works the instrument and slowly revolves it, he forces the metal downward and inward, carefully and evenly.

After the rim has been bent to a certain point, the glass slips down when the instrument is removed, and the performer carefully takes it from the frame. Then he is free to open the top of the tube. Replacing the glass and bending the bottom of the tube back into position is not a difficult process, especially as the performer may have any necessary tools in the cabinet. This brings the whole arrangement back to its original condition, and the escape comes to a successful conclusion. Removing the glass is slower than crushing it, but as the performer has plenty of time in which to accomplish the escape, it is difficult to decide which of the two methods has the greater merit. That is a matter which only experiment could prove; all other factors being equal, removal of the glass would be preferable. The substitution of duplicate parts in something to be avoided whenever possible, and the last method explained eliminates such an action.

ESCAPE FROM A BLOCK OF ICE

In this unusual escape the performer is imprisoned in a covered iron cylinder which is effectively closed from the top. A huge block of ice, hollowed in the center, is placed over the cylinder and comes down to the platform, which is raised from the stage. Hence the man inside must not only escape from the cylinder; he must also overcome the heavy cake of ice. The cover that fits on the cylinder is not hinged; it is fitted with hasps that fit over staples on the cylinder, and it cannot be removed by any usual method after the cake of ice is in position.

The secret of this escape lies in the construction of the cylinder, which has very thick walls and will stand a close inspection. The thick wall is really three layers of metal. First a thin cylinder with solid bottom is constructed, and a hole is cut in the side above the bottom. The hole is large enough for a person to pass through. Then a double cylinder or shell is made; it has no bottom, and its walls are several inches apart, being closed at the top. This fits over the original cylinder, and when it is in position it hides the secret opening both inside and outside. By lifting this shell, the opening is revealed and the performer can make use of it. If desired, short bolts may pass through the inner wall of the shell into the genuine cylinder and thus prevent any one from lifting the shell; if a tight fit of shell and cylinder is obtained, this is hardly necessary. But assuming that the bolts are used, their removal and replacement from the inside will free the shell, and the performer can raise it. The great difficulty then is the cake of ice. It is so heavy that even if the performer can raise it, he cannot hold it up while he makes his escape. That is why the ice is used—to direct suspicion away from the true secret of the iron cylinder.

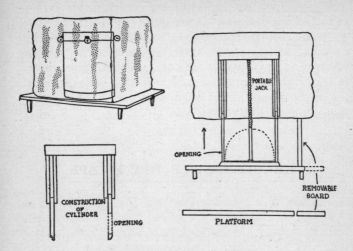

HOW THE CYLINDER IS COVERED
WITH THE BLOCK OF ICE; ALSO CONSTRUCTION
OF THE CYLINDER AND DETAILS
OF THE ESCAPE

When the performer enters the cylinder he carries a jack concealed on his person. Inside the cylinder he fits this jack together and uses it to raise the shell and the cake of ice. The sides of the cake of ice make it really an outer shell. Then the performer comes out through the opening. He can lower the jack from below, but this has two disadvantages; it is not only a difficult process, but it leaves the jack inside the cylinder at the finish. To overcome this the ends of the platform are used. They are removable, and the performer places them so that they will block the outer shell and the cake of ice as they are lowered by the jack. Having made his escape, he puts the end boards of the platform in position, drops the jack and removes it, and then knocks the boards out of the way so that the shell and the cake of ice come down to the platform. The ends of the platform are replaced, the jack is concealed, and everything is ready for the committee. When the jack is raised it presses against the inside of the cover, which is attached to the outer part of the shell. The center cylinder does not need to extend clear to the top of the shell; hence the staples for the locks can be bolted or riveted all the way through. It is advisable to have an air-hole in the center of the cover, with a corresponding hole in the center of the cake of ice, as the escape is not a rapid one and the performer will need air.

THE AUTOMOBILE TIRE ESCAPE

An escape from a large automobile tire, mounted on a rim, while the wheel is revolving! This is an idea that has spectacular possibilities. The wheel used is very large; the tire is cut before the escape begins, so that the performer may be imprisoned in it. Then the tire is mounted on the wheel and the ends are vulcanized. The performer obtains air through holes in the tire. The whole wheel is slowly revolved; the curtains of the cabinet are closed, but a space is left open so that the spectators can observe the hub of the wheel as it continues to revolve. The whole tire is set in a special stand that makes this possible, and a belt is connected to a flange on the rim of the wheel so as to keep it in revolution. The wheel, however, does not revolve while the performer is making his escape. The extending hub is large and the end runs independently—the notes suggest the use of clock-work. The belt running to the rim of the wheel is secretly disconnected by an assistant, so the performer can get out of the tire while it is standing still.

Two methods are suggested for this escape. One is to cut the large tire at the point where it has been vulcanized. The performer does this with a sharp knife, and eventually breaks loose. He replaces the tire on the stand, and with a small vulcanizing outfit which has been hidden in the cabinet, he repairs the damage.

The other method depends on a trap in the tire itself. This is a flap, with edges cut at an angle so that it fits very nicely. The trap is four-sided, one side being uncut; this acts as a hinge. The flap is cemented in position before the escape; thus the tire will stand considerable examination. The performer uses a special knife or spatula with which he can do a very neat job of cutting, simply prying loose the flap where it is cemented, without injuring the rubber. Then he can open the long flap and make his escape. The secret trap must then be cemented back into its original position. With a very large tire, this method would not require the vulcanizing of loose ends; the performer would find it possible to enter the tire while it was in its normal shape. Hence it is quicker both as a presentation and as an escape, and is preferable to the vulcanizing method, provided that the cemented flap will pass inspection.

THE MAINE TRAMP CHAIR

Houdini's notebook contains photographs of the Maine tramp chair, a device that was once employed to confine tramps or suspicious characters overnight. The escape from this contrivance was introduced by Hardeen, the brother of Houdini, who performed it in Bangor, Maine, accomplishing it in eleven minutes. Houdini's notes state that Hardeen employed the escape and also mention that Houdini did it in Boston and called it the witch's chair. The tramp chair forms a miniature portable cell; it consists of two sections, the lower cubical in shape, the upper square-bottomed but high, so that the prisoner may be seated in the chair-like interior. When the door is closed, the open side is fastened by a padlock over a staple. The door is located in the upper portion of the chair, and a long, heavy pivot hinge holds it to the framework of the cell. The fact that the

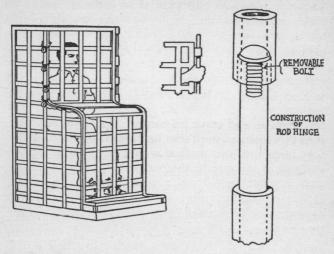

REMOVABLE BOLT

CONSTRUCTION OF ROD HINGE

**SKETCH OF THE MAINE TRAMP CHAIR
WITH DETAILS OF THE ESCAPE**

device was used to imprison dangerous characters is sufficient proof of its formidable construction.

Houdini's notes do not contain an explanation of the working method of the tramp chair as used either by himself or by Hardeen. There is, however, a method of preparing a chair of this type so that the performer can make an effective escape; yet the device will stand close inspection. The secret lies in the long pivot hinge that holds the door of the chair in position. The hinge cannot be removed because of plugs in the top and bottom sockets. Without these plugs, it would be impossible to push the rod downward because of the bottom portion of the chair. The top plug may be removed, yet still the hinge cannot be pushed upward because the upper portion of the hole in the top socket is too small for it. But when the performer is ready to escape, he reaches out from the chair and removes the plugs from the upper and lower sockets. Then he draws the rod downward, and it goes far enough to free the top end from the upper socket. The top of the rod thus revealed is fitted with a screw-bolt; the performer removes this, and the rod is then free to pass upward through the sockets. The rod is small enough to go through the upper socket; its not moving upward when tested is due to the head of the bolt, which is of greater diameter than the rod.

The ingenuity of this method is obvious. Committee-men who suspect the hinge are easily convinced that the rod will not go downward more than a few inches; hence the only plug that they will insist on removing is the top one. With the plug out of the way, it is still quite impossible to budge the rod. The double action of moving the rod downward and then upward is some-thing that no one will suspect; this makes the escape from the prepared or faked tramp chair a highly con-vincing mystery. When the performer makes his exit, the padlocked side of the door serves as a hinge. To show the escape most effectively, he may allow chains to be passed through the network of bars, at the pad-locked side of the door. The chains may be equipped with padlocks supplied by members of the committee and may be firmly fastened, for they merely add to the security of the side that is not opened. This method is usable when the escape is made with the performer's own apparatus, as part of a regular performance. Har-deen's escape in Bangor was made from an old tramp chair in the possession of the police of that city, and he performed it as a challenge. Hence the method that he used was necessarily different from the one described here.

An illusion, rather than an escape, the knife box presents an unusual problem for the performer who is placed within it. The box is an upright cabinet with a door that opens outward. The interior is filled with knives projecting from the sides and the back; when the performer is placed in the box and the door is closed, there is very little room for him to move about in without injury. He is placed in the cabinet upside down, naturally this adds to his difficulties. Then the box is attached to a chain and is lifted in the air. It does not leave the view of the audience; but when the box is lowered and reopened, the performer is standing upright! In some unaccountable manner he has managed to change his position despite the knives.

This trick is included among Houdini's escapes because it is a mystery involving the confinement of the performer in a box; and with certain modifications it could be used as an escape behind curtains. The box is large enough to permit the performer to turn over; the problem that must be overcome is that of the knives, which actually prevent motion and are genuine blades. These knives are set on hinges in the sides and back of the box; but this fact is not observed, for the knives are actually attached to plates which appear to be screwed into the wood. Hence, as the notes say, the "knives are shown 'not hinged.'" But the plates or attachments for the knives are fitted to round joint hinges in the walls of the box. The result is that all of the knives can be folded flat against the sides and back of the box, releasing the performer.

To accomplish this, Houdini planned an interior mechanism that is not given in detail. When the box is examined the knives cannot be moved, and the performer, when confined, is unable to turn the knives himself; hence the box will stand the most thorough examination. The release lies in a handle or group of handles on the outside of the box—evidently at the top. These handles pull upward, and when they do, the knives swing flat against the walls of the box. The release is actuated by the simple process of raising the cabinet. Chains are attached to the handles after the door is closed. The chains are drawn tight, and they pull the handles upward for a short distance before the handles actually begin to raise the box. The weight of the box and the performer resist the pull and make this automatic. So as soon as the box is in the air the knives are out of the way and the performer can eaily turn over and take his standing position. When the box is lowered, the knives come back into place as soon as it strikes the floor and the chains fall loose or become slack.

The effectiveness of this trick depends largely on its construction. It must be well made mechanically; yet there is no reason why the apparatus should be complicated to any excessive degree. As a self-working device it is ingenious. Some arrangement would probably be necessary to hold the performer in his upside-down position until the box is raised and the knives are out of the way. The release of the knives is clever, as there is nothing suspicious about it. It is quite logical that the box should be opened and closed while on the stage; raising it in the air seems obviously a plan to make the trick more difficult—instead of making it easy. The box can be lifted the instant the door is closed and reopened just as soon as it comes back to the stage. The change can be made in very quick order. All in all, this appears to be a practical and effective illusion that can be presented in a sensational manner.

THE SPIRIT COLLAR

The collar here described is as much a trick as an escape, and it is a very effective mystery, as the articles used are entirely unprepared. Houdini describes it in a note dated October 26, 1904:

"The collar is made in the shape of an ice-pick, and the rivet can be examined and a new one put in at every show. The lock can be sealed up, but still the collar is removed from the neck, and seals are unbroken.

"The secret: A certain part of the neck is very thin; if you put one point of the collar under your chin near your ear, you can force it way into your neck and you will be able to work the collar from your neck."

A diagram follows the explanation; it shows that the points of the collar have small caps on them, which of course protect the performer. The collar, as described and drawn, is shaped like an ice-pick, with the handles locked; the points of the pick come very close together, and it appears impossible that the collar could be removed from the neck. By gaining as much distance as possible between the points and carefully manipulating the collar, the performer can easily work it free.

THE CHAMPION LOCK CUFF

Houdini terms this "a splendid freak cuff," and mentions it both in his notebook and in miscellaneous notes. It is a very formidable device, and yet escape from it is simple.

The cuff consists of a long heavy bolt, with a hole in the end. Houdini states that it "is made on the style of the Russian cuffs, like those in Scotland Yard; two bands for hands; the bands are then placed through the

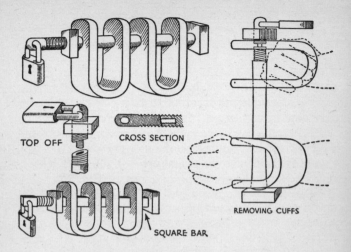

TOP OFF   CROSS SECTION

SQUARE BAR

REMOVING CUFFS

OPERATION OF THE CHAMPION LOCK CUFF.
TWO STYLES (ROUND BAR AND SQUARE BAR)
ARE SHOWN

rod. Any lock can be hung on, and still escape can be made." The explanation follows:

"Have the holes in the hand loops square, or of some eccentric form. The long bar screws in the center, and is also made square, which allows the hands to unscrew the long bar and take it apart.

"It would be safest to have a round bar with an eccentric bump which would unscrew the bar.

"Another method is to have the bolt-head unscrew; it fits into a key (plate with square hole) that is fixed in the cabinet, to hold it steady while the head is being taken off.

"This can be made into a very sensational-looking cuff, by making use of a very heavy piece of steel for the bar. It should be as weighty as possible; and to show that these cuffs are not slipped it is wise to have a pair of ratchet cuffs on the wrists at the same time."

The ratchet cuffs would, of course, be nearer the

hands than the special cuffs; they would be removed with the aid of a key. It is understood that the performer fits the long bolt together after the escape.

TWO TRICKY DOORS

The "tricky" doors are not used in escapes; they are intended as mysterious devices that will perplex the uninitiated, and they are very ingenious in their construction. These doors cannot be opened by any one who does not know the secret. The first door cannot be shown open at all, for it opens at the hinges and not at the lock. It has dummy hinges at the left and a dummy lock at the right. It is hinged at the right by two rods, one at the top, the other at the bottom. These fit into the woodwork above and below the doorway and act as pivot hinges. At the left of the door a similar rod is

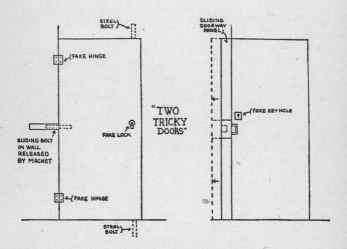

**DIAGRAMS EXPLAINING THE OPERATION
OF THE TRICKY DOORS**

concealed in both the door and the woodwork of the doorway, but it is in a horizontal instead of a vertical position.

The man who attempts to open this door will find a real problem confronting him. He cannot pick the lock, for it is useless; pushing the pins from the hinges will be to no avail, for the door will still be solid at that side. The only way to open the door is with the aid of a powerful magnet. This is applied to the woodwork at the left; then it is moved to the right. The rod at the left is not as long as the slots in which it is fitted; so with the magnet working it moves to the right into the door (or it can be drawn into the woodwork at the left); and this makes the opening a simple matter because of the pivot hinges at the right!

The second door can be shown either open or closed. It has a lock that is permanently closed and cannot be picked. When the door is open, this lock is still closed; that is, the metal part is extending from the door. The box into which this permanent lock is fitted is attached to the woodwork at the side of the door. If the woodwork is removed, the door will open when pulled, for there will be nothing there to hold the lock. Instead of having to remove the woodwork of the doorway, the performer merely slides it away from the door. The whole vertical piece slides, in grooves at the top of the doorway and in the floor. This is concealed by molding at the top and on the baseboard of the floor. This door is not so ingenious nor so perfect as the one previously described, but it is much more easily constructed, as the door is simply put in position and the woodwork of the doorway fitted afterward. It is easy to operate, requires no tool or magnet, and is so cleverly devised that detection is very unlikely.

Houdini's method of escaping from a large valise, described in notes dated July 12, 1910, at Chicago, depended on a valise which was not specially prepared, but which required certain specifications in its construction. The valise would have to be made very large, to allow considerable space in which the performer could move; and air-holes were also mentioned in the notes. The method of escape can be understood from a description of the valise. The bag is held by two pairs of straps, the ends of the straps being riveted to the bottom of the valise. The description of one pair of straps shows that one strap is fastened near the front of the bottom, the other strap near the rear of the bottom.

With the performer inside the bag, the front strap is drawn up and its free end pushed through a buckle on the free end of the rear strap. By having a short rear strap, the front strap can be inserted through staples on the top of the bag before it is put through the buckle of the rear strap. A padlock pushed through a metal-rimmed hole in the front strap is the means by which the straps are held together; the padlock obviously cannot be pulled through the buckle. With members of the audience examining and locking the valise, this is a highly convincing escape that seems to border on the impossible.

The method of escape is to work on the rivets of the front strap. By cutting these from the inside of the bag, the strap is released, and by pressing in opposite directions at the top of the bag, an opening is gained through which the performer can pull the strap entirely clear. As two sets of straps are used it is necessary to cut two groups of rivets and to operate both straps simultaneously. The fact that the front straps were marked as the ones to be released indicates that the use of staples on

the top of the bag was intended. The release of the rear
straps would not be effective, as the buckles could not
pass through the staples.

Provision is made for clamps on the metal-work of
the rim of the valise; these, however, must be of a
standard pattern. Most clamps of this sort, no matter
how impressive they may appear, can be easily forced
from the inside. The object is to have regulation clamps
which seem to add to the security of the valise, yet
which offer no great difficulty to the man inside. The
clamps are forced open in order to manipulate the top
of the valise and release the straps. The use of a small
tool to operate the clamps is not an obstacle, as the
performer must carry an instrument to cut the rivets,
either hiding it on his person or having it concealed in
the valise. When the performer is out of the valise he
replaces the cut rivets with new ones. This is accomplished most effectively by opening the locks with a key
or a pick, thus releasing the front straps, which are
refastened after the rivets have been put in place. In an
emergency the rivets can be inserted after the bag is
closed, without access to the interior; in this case, only
a casual inspection may be made after the escape.

Part Eight

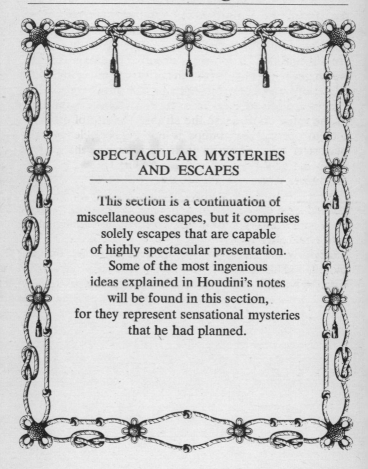

SPECTACULAR MYSTERIES
AND ESCAPES

This section is a continuation of
miscellaneous escapes, but it comprises
solely escapes that are capable
of highly spectacular presentation.
Some of the most ingenious
ideas explained in Houdini's notes
will be found in this section,
for they represent sensational mysteries
that he had planned.

An escape from a cradle of steel, while suspended from the top, was one of the challenges proposed by Houdini. It possesses the elements of a spectacular escape. The cradle is mounted on a platform. It consists of four upright posts supporting a solid top, all of heavy construction. Metal plates in the top hold rings, one to support the performer's neck, another for his body, the third for his ankles. A metal collar is placed about the performer's neck; it is locked and secured to the ring in the top of the cradle by a chain. A strip of steel belting, attached to the center ring and locked there, holds his body. His feet are secured by a leather strap or by a piece of metal made like a figure 8 which closes over each ankle independently and can be locked to the ring above.

The notes state that the arms are held by steel tubing; no details are given of this apparatus. An additional note describes a pair of cuffs or manacles connected by a chain; these are evidently the device to be used in securing the performer's wrists. The escape depends on releasing the hands. The manacles used are not faked, but the hinge of each one is simply a rivet on which the bars swing. After the performer is in position, and securely attached to the cradle, the curtains are lowered and he starts to work, using a pair of plier-like cutters concealed on his person.

Resting easily in the cradle-like device, he releases his hands. With the manacles in use, the chain between them allows plenty of space for one hand to work on the opposite wrist. With a hand free, the performer reaches to the neck strap and cuts the zinc rivet that supports it. He can support his body by holding the other ring with his free hand. The steel belting offers no resistance. It is tight, but it cannot hold the performer's body, for the belting is pliable. Hence the remainder of the escape depends on the release of the feet. Bound in a broad strap of leather, the feet can be slipped if they have been crossed in fastening. Otherwise the performer must work his way forward, raising his knees and extending his hands until he can reach his feet. If the feet are fastened with a leather strap, the performer cuts the strap. If they are in the figure 8 device, he must use the cutters once more, to remove a rivet at the bottom of the figure 8. In brief, the method is to release the neck and the ankles, then slide free from the body belt. Free, the performer must replace everything that he has cut—either rivet or strap.

This is an escape that is not so difficult as it appears to the audience, yet not so easy as it may seem from the explanation. Working on rivets that are out of sight and difficult to reach requires both skill and patience. Only an experienced performer could attempt this escape, and in devising it, Houdini relied on his proven ability.

WALKING THROUGH A BRICK WALL

The mysterious feat of walking through a brick wall was not one of Houdini's originations, but it has become closely identified with his name, for he introduced the illusion to the American stage and presented it with remarkable success. It was an ideal feat for Houdini to perform, for it can be classed both as a magical illusion and as an escape trick; and Houdini's popular reputation was certain to be an attraction for so sensational a mystery.

The wall was built of brick on an iron framework some twelve feet in length. The framework was mounted on rollers so that it could be moved about the stage, and in its final position it stood with one end toward the audience. A committee was invited on to the stage. The inspection proved conclusively that the wall was just what it appeared to be—a solid structure of

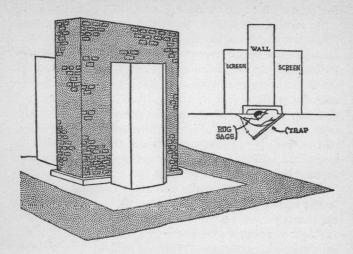

**WALKING THROUGH A BRICK WALL.—
ONE OF HOUDINI'S MOST FAMOUS MYSTERIES**

brick; in fact, the wall could be built in the presence of the audience, if desired. The stage also bore minute inspection. It was covered with a large carpet of plain design and of heavy material, precluding all possibility of any openings. To make everything more convincing, a large cloth, inspected by the committee, was spread over the carpet. Then the brick wall was set in the center of the stage, and two threefold screens were placed against it, one on each side of the wall.

Houdini went behind one of the screens, while the committee members stood on all sides, watching the wall from every angle. Houdini raised his hands above the screen for a moment; then drew them within the screen. The seconds clicked by, and suddenly the screen on the other side of the wall was moved away, and there stood the performer! When the first screen was taken down, it proved to be empty. Thus Houdini apparently passed through a solid brick wall, some eight feet in height, under the most exacting conditions.

This effect seemed miraculous, as it was apparently impossible for the performer to go through, over, around, or beneath the wall. Under it would have seemed most logical, but with only five or six inches of space and the carpet and cloth preventing use of a trapdoor, that method of passage seemed unusable. Yet Houdini went *underneath* the wall.

A large trapdoor was set in the center of the stage. When the screens were in position, the door was opened from below. Both the cloth and the carpet, which were large in area, sagged with the weight of the performer's body, allowing sufficient space for him to work his way through, the cloth yielding as he progressed. The passage accomplished, the trap was closed, and no clue remained.

Even with people standing on the cloth, the "give" in the center was quite unnoticeable, and the passage from one side of the wall to the other was quickly accomplished by a man of Houdini's agility.

WALLED IN ALIVE!

One of the most ambitious escapes planned by Houdini was the "walled-in alive" test. It is very carefully described in his notes, and Houdini gives the effect in his own words:

"The idea is to have on the stage, raised from the floor, extra heavy horses of wood, to support a heavy plate of warship steel. On this is to be plastered a flooring of concrete and huge paving bricks, or rocks, the large square kind.

"The masons start to build up a wall, forming a room, and after it is a certain height, I enter and am walled in.

"It cannot be air-tight, so a cross-shaped opening is left at the top or the side, to admit air. After the whole thing is walled up and I am inside, if I were to attempt

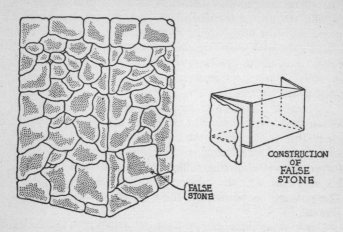

FALSE STONE

CONSTRUCTION
OF
FALSE
STONE

**SECTION OF SOLID WALL SHOWING
THE LOCATION AND CONSTRUCTION OF FALSE STONE
THROUGH WHICH THE PERFORMER PASSES**

to remove a solitary stone, all would tumble down. The curtain is drawn around, and within a certain time limit, I escape, leaving the 'buried alive' chamber intact."

Some details are missing from Houdini's description, but they are easily supplied. The opening in the wall is, of course, too small to be of any use in the escape. The top of the structure would probably require another sheet of steel, covered with stones; but with a high wall, this would be unnecessary, as the wall could project above the curtain, so any attempt to climb over the top would be detected. This plan would eliminate the necessity for an air-hole. As Houdini stated, any attempt to remove a stone from any part of the wall would be disastrous. The ingenious method he created made it absolutely unnecessary to remove any stone; in fact the size and weight of the stones is of value in the escape. The secret lies in one stone, which is specially prepared. Houdini's original plan was to have a large hollowed stone, with the ends filled with a plaster to make it look unprepared. The interior of the stone was to hold tools and fresh plaster; so when he broke into the stone and forced his way through it, he would have the materials to repair the damage.

This being rather cumbersome, he improved the method, using a steel box instead of the hollow stone. The box is covered with stone or an artificial stone surface, so that it closely resembles a genuine stone. It has snap doors in each end, with handles on the insides. The only implement needed by the performer is a small key or tool to open the inner door. After making his passage through the fake stone, he closes the doors. In case plaster is needed in the crevices on the other side of the stone, the necessary material can be kept in the hollow block; and any repair work would be a matter of a very few minutes.

Houdini's diagram calls for the "stone" to be set near the bottom of the wall. Obviously it would have to be large, and the real blocks would be of the same size, with smaller stones for higher portions of the wall. With so many stones required, and the building of the wall being a matter requiring speed, the imitation stone can easily pass the cursory inspection of the committee. Stones of this size are convincing because of their size and weight, and their use is logical in a large wall that must be quickly built. The plan of passing through a solid stone is certainly the last mode of exit that any one would suspect.

THE CYLINDRICAL CROSS ESCAPE

There is a certain parallel between Houdini's theatrical career and the various notes that he made of new ideas. Notes on escapes from ordinary objects such as baskets and barrels bear dates before 1910; the more spectacular tricks are of slightly later date. This conforms with his introduction of the sensational water-torture cell, which was not part of his earlier programs. It seems as though his inventive talents were first applied to devising a variety of smaller or lesser escapes, later to the creation of feature mysteries that could be exhibited almost as an act in themselves. For Houdini was a progressive showman, not content to rest on the laurels of the past, and he had plans for the development of new and spectacular ideas.

The escape from a cylindrical cross stands out as a masterpiece of ingenuity. Its construction would probably have been a matter of great expense; presented as a feature escape, it would have been sensational. The notes on this escape were written while crossing the Atlantic on board the North German Lloyd steamer *Kaiser Wilhelm II*; they are dated August 29 and August 30, 1912. The apparatus planned by Houdini was a cross-shaped device made of metal tubing. This was designed to break apart in the center, along the horizontal tube. Thus the cross consisted of two portions, each shaped like the letter T. The base of each T was a round tube, the top a half tube. One tube was to set right side up, the other to be inverted.

Let us visualize this escape as the audience would see it. A committee is invited on the stage. They examine both sections of the strange cylindrical cross. The two parts are similar, but one stands higher than the other. The ends of the vertical tubes are closed, solidly riveted in place. The performer steps into the taller portion of the cross; it comes up to his arms, and he lays each arm in the trough or half-circle extending from each side of the center section. Attention is called to the fact that there is just about enough space for the lower part of his body. Then the other portion of the cross is turned upside down and set over his head. The horizontal half-tubes correspond exactly to those of the lower section, so the performer is contained in a cross made of cylinders. The arm sections have flanges. These are provided with holes, and bolts or padlocks are fitted so that the

NORDDEUTSCHER LLOYD
BREMEN.

On board

D. „KAISER WILHELM I°

aug 29/50 —12

Escape from of cylindrical cross

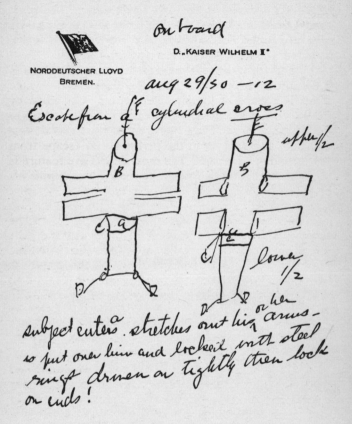

subject enters. stretches out his or her arms.
is put over him and locked with steel
rings driven on tightly then lock
on ends!

REPRODUCTION OF HOUDINI'S FIRST NOTES
ON THE CYLINDRICAL CROSS ESCAPE. THIS IS A
TYPICAL SPECIMEN OF THE MATERIAL
FROM WHICH THIS VOLUME WAS PREPARED

two portions of the cross may be tightly fastened together. When this has been done, the performer is as effectively secured as any one could desire. The horizontal tubes are longer than his arms so that his hands cannot emerge; his body has very little space in which to move. In fact, the performer appears helpless.

To add to the effectiveness of this escape, a chain is fitted into a swivel at the top of the cross and the whole affair is hoisted in the air. The bottom is steadied by chains that serve as guy-ropes; these are hitched to hooks in the floor. The hanging cross is surrounded by curtains, and it is up to the performer to escape from his formidable restraint. The most impressive feature is the fact that he cannot move; no matter how supple his body might be, it would be impossible for him to wiggle clear of the device. To prevent the one possible method —a method possible only in theory—namely, escape through an arm hole, the ends of the horizontal tube are also closed and held by bolts. All the ends stand the most thorough inspection; all parts of the cross are reënforced by thick metal bands; and the committee and the audience both are positive that only a miracle can help the performer to extricate himself from the device. Yet he gets out, and the cylindrical cross is found in exactly the same position as before, the bolts intact, and the device ready for thorough inspection!

This was indeed an escape worthy of Houdini; had he constructed it and shown it in public it would have created a tremendous sensation. The secret is extremely ingenious; Houdini appears to have hit on the only solution workable with such a device, with the conditions exactly as described—the ends of each section positively solid; the bolts genuine, and no end of the cross reachable with his hands. The vulnerable point of this device lies directly beneath the horizontal cylinder. This point is necessarily reënforced by a metal band or connecting joint which holds the horizontal cylinder to the bottom part. The rivets here are genuine. The same method of connection is used between the horizontal cylinder and the upper section, but that point is not vulnerable.

Note how the cross is suspended. The top is attached to a swivel; the bottom is held firm by two or more guy-lines. It is apparently impossible for the performer to move within the cylindrical cross. Yet he does move; not upward, downward, or sideways, but by a rotary motion, turning around. He manages to do this because at the bottom of the connection between the base of the cross and the horizontal cylinder, the base of the cross is fitted with a threaded screw! This is a tight fit, a close joint that cannot be detected; it withstands all strain and holds the sections of the base firmly together; best of all, it is something that no one would begin to suspect!

As soon as the cross is screened from view, the performer begins to turn. The bottom of the cross is firmly held; the performer's arms, in their metal casings, act as powerful levers. The swivel at the top allows that section of the cross to revolve. Everything is taut. Around goes the performer, and the unseen joint unscrews. Finally he reaches the end; the bottom falls free; and he is hanging by his extended arms. The dimensions of the cylinders are of corresponding size. This factor now comes to the performer's advantage. He is able to do something that would not have been possible with the cross closed; namely, he can draw in his arms, one at a time, by letting his body slip downward. Before, the base of the cross prevented this; now it can be done. Hence by using some agility, the performer extricates himself from the upper portion of the cross. His next task is to replace the bottom. To accomplish this he should have a chair or some object in the cabinet, as he cannot hold the lower section in the air and revolve the upper portion at the same time. Lowering the chain is an alternative; this can be done if the chain runs through a loop inside the cabinet and is attached to the floor. Either is a minor point that is not difficult to manage. The important item is that the performer sets

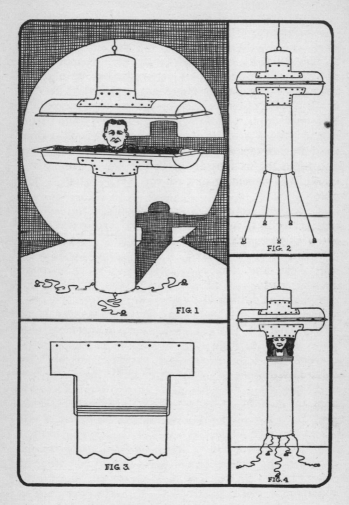

DETAILS OF THE CYLINDRICAL CROSS ESCAPE

the two portions of the cross together and screws them back into position, then leaves everything exactly as it was before the escape.

When the curtains are withdrawn the cross is hanging there as mysterious as ever, and the committee can examine the bolts and every part of the apparatus. The guy-ropes are released and the cross is brought down to the floor. It should be noted that when the cross is loose, unscrewing the two portions is virtually impossible. The bottom portion must be firmly held in order to turn the upper section. The apparatus requires that the top be free to turn while the bottom is held in position. Even inside the cross the secret cannot be discovered, for the necessary leverage to turn the tight-fitting screw cannot be obtained. Any rotary motion inside the free cross would merely upset the device. One or two men would have to hold the base while two others pushed the arms in the required direction. There is no danger of this, for the secret is too ingenious to excite suspicion, and coöperative energy on the part of committee-men is easily overcome.

Considered from every standpoint, this is as nearly perfect as an escape can be. It is a device with remarkable possibilities. Devices built by an escape artist and introduced by him must be formidable and capable of standing the closest examination; the cylindrical cross meets both requirements to perfection. The reader will appreciate that a contrivance of this sort must be well made in every detail. It is difficult to estimate the cost of its construction, but it is safe to say that it could not be manufactured cheaply. Whatever the expense, a trick like this is worth it. There are few escapes convincing enough and spectacular enough to be exhibited as an entire program in themselves; the cylindrical cross is one of these few. It ranks with Houdini's water-torture cell and can certainly be classed as one of his greatest and most ingenious creations.

THE SUSPENDED BRASS TUBE

The instructions for this escape were written by Houdini on September 1, 1912, two days after he had drawn diagrams and sketches for the cylindrical cross escape. There are certain points of similarity in the two ideas, but the methods of operation are quite different. Both are spectacular escapes. Houdini planned that the brass tube should be built to fit a regulation porthole; this indicates that he evolved the idea aboard the steamship. He also planned that the end of the tube (that is, the top) should contain a sheet of glass.

The effect of the escape is as follows:

The performer exhibits a large brass tube into which his body will fit so tightly that very little motion is possible, even to the extent of raising the arms. The bottom of the tube is a heavy brass cover, riveted to the tube itself. The top is a detachable cover, designed like a porthole, which may be clamped tightly in place. There are hooks or rings in both top and bottom, so that the tube may be suspended between two chains. The committee examines everything. All parts of the tube stand rigid inspection and pressure. The performer enters head first, so that he cannot possibly use his hands to work on the cover; but when the cover is fitted into place, it is so solidly bolted and clamped by a flange provided with holes that every one is positive that inside operation is impossible anyhow. If glass is used in the top, it differentiates the top from the bottom, and also enables the committee-men to see the performer's feet after he has been placed within. Heavy chains are attached to both ends of the tube. The bottom chain is fastened to a metal ring in the stage; the upper end is carried over a pulley on a solid framework and continues off-stage. The result is that the tube is suspended at an angle between the two taut chains and

the performer has to make his escape from that difficult position.

The method of release is entirely different from most
others, for this is one escape in which the performer is
dependent on outside assistance. The bottom of the
tube is removable. The rivets on the outside are false;
they do not go entirely through the tube. But the bottom fits very tight, so tight in fact that no one can push
or pull it loose. The ends of the false rivets hold it
firmly in position. Even inside the tube, the performer
is helpless; the tube is so long that his feet do not reach
the top; his hands are at his sides, and there is no way
in which he can exert pressure to push the bottom from
the tube. How then, does he escape? The release is
effected off stage!

The chain that holds the top of the tube passes off
stage and is wound around a winch. The assistant uses
this to tighten the chain before the cabinet is placed
around the suspended brass tube. As soon as the curtains are closed, the assistant, who has not drawn the
chain to its greatest tightness—he may still be winding
the winch slowly when the cabinet is put in position—
turns the winch farther. The chains, the hooks on the
tube, and the ring in the floor are all considerably
stronger than the fastenings of the removable bottom.
As a result, the tightening of the winch pulls the brass
tube apart. The bottom drops off, and the chain remains straight because of the weight of the upper portion, which swings down to the stage. This enables the
performer to slide right out of the tube. He puts the
apparatus back into its original condition by setting the
tube on the bottom and hammering it down into position so that it will again pass examination. The greater
part of the work lies in fixing the tube after the escape;
the release itself is a matter of a very few seconds.

There are, of course, certain details to be considered.
The chain that goes off stage must not betray what is
going on within the cabinet. In replacing the tube, the

performer can unhook the bottom and move it over to a spot below the tube; he will require some slack in the chain to hook the apparatus back in position, but this can be given gradually. The upper chain can be entirely masked outside of the cabinet, passing behind a scene or a wing; even if visible, slight motion of the chain is not suspicious.

Having decided on this method of escape, Houdini followed with rough plans to work the trick while the tube was filled with water. The required details of this improvement are not complete. The pull-off method was the same, but certain difficulties presented themselves, and these are not entirely solved. The close-fitting bottom of the tube could hold water. The difficulty lay in going into the tube head first, and having the bottom operate as usual; for with this procedure the water would come out before the performer! So Houdini planned an upright stand with swivels fitting into projections on the side of the tube. Here the tube would hang free; apparently to prevent the performer from swinging it, chains would be attached, running off stage —probably to the back, or else to opposite sides.

The arrangement of these chains provided that the upper chain should go down to the floor, while the lower chain would go through a framework above. Tightening the chains would thus have two effects, first to swing the tube on the swivel in the stand so that the bottom would come up to the top and the performer would be head first. The tight-fitting porthole would prevent water from escaping. Further tightening of the chains would then cause the bottom of the tube to pop off in an upward direction. The performer would require sufficient space to move one arm, so that he could either hold to a cross-bar inside the bottom and be drawn with it, or could work his way upward by reaching the edge of the tube. No water would escape; and when the performer had emerged, he could replace the false bottom and jam it into position from the top of the heavy stand. Then by a signal along the chain, the assistants would know when to release the chains letting the tube back to its original position.

It is obvious that this more elaborate escape, while possibly workable, involves many complications in an effect which is ideally simple in its original form. It illustrates very clearly why every feat of magic, escapes included, should avoid difficult systems of operation. It is rather doubtful whether the added effect of having water in the can is worth the extra preparation, especially as the use of the chains becomes suspicious rather than natural. Nevertheless, Houdini possessed the ability to smooth out such difficulties and to make complicated arrangements simple. Having devised a new escape, he invariably found the most satisfactory form in which to present it. With the brass tube escape, he would either have shown it without the water and would have made it a very spectacular effect, or he would eventually have developed the reversing of the tube and the upward pull into a practical method that would have deceived the most critical observers.

THE GREAT CELL MYSTERY

The description and explanation of this cell mystery are quoted from Houdini's notes on the escape, which are considerably detailed. It is an effective mystery that involves a very unusual principle.

"The cell is large and lined with steel or aluminum. The man is locked in, and from the inside it is absolutely impossible for any one to help himself. The locks are on the outside and there is to be no trap, no faked rivets or faked hinges.

"Then the cell will be either chained or roped as with the trunk escape. After a few minutes the man is free.

"The secret: The locks are to be made of a special pattern. Each lock looks exactly like a very fine Chubb;

in fact it is to be a complicated lever lock the same as used on a safe.

"But it is to be made to open from the inside, with a strong electro-magnet!

"The committee has one key, but this locks twice, and when the lock is locked twice, no man can get out, as the magnet will not work. This is so that a reward can be offered to any one that can get out. I am to do it first and can then change the lock so that a magnet will not work.

"But the safest way is to have a triple lock, and the committee holds the key which locks twice; or if possible have it lock four times: then the committee can lock it twice.

"The door should be held inside by a rather long sheet of steel, which prevents it from coming in; but when this sheet of steel is removed from the inside, it will allow the door to come in just far enough to allow me to squeeze out; or the door may be made so that after the lock is open, you can lift it up from the inside, and thus allow it to be easily pulled inward. Then the closing is easy enough. This must be made to work very quickly.

"The sheet of steel that prevents the door from closing can be made of malleable steel, which only a strong instrument can bend; and this can be bent out of the way of the door. This will not allow the cell to be examined afterward, but it is a good thing to remember.

"This mystery, worked properly, ought to be a great advertising scheme. Advertised as a new system of mystery: no faked hinges, no faked screws. Offer a reward to any one who can find his way out, or can find that the cell is not properly made.

"It would be a good idea to use a good straitjacket and be strapped inside the cell, and then get out of both. This can easily be done by working the straitjacket like I worked it with Circus Carré. While they are securing the cell outside, this would allow ample time to release myself from the jacket.

"An idea is to have a bolt on the cell, arranged so that by removing a small screw, a stiffened wire may be inserted; pushing the wire will release a powerful spring that will pull back the bolt.

"This can easily be arranged so that it can never come back by accident, but will require pressure. When pressure is released it will relock."

The novel part of this escape is the use of the lock that can be opened with a magnet. Such an ingenious contrivance would never be suspected, but it is interesting to note that Houdini intended to make the lock absolutely certain in case any one else should attempt to escape from the cell. Houdini refers to more than one lock at the beginning of the description and later speaks of a single lock; this means, of course, that any additional locks would operate alike. The door is evidently intended to open outward; secured with chains or ropes, it could not be pushed open; hence the necessity for bringing the door inward far enough to slip through the opening. The replacement of the steel sheet that prevents the door from coming inward is not entirely clear in the explanation, and there are no diagrams accompanying the notes. This, however, is not the important factor of the mystery, and it is evident that Houdini planned some simple and practical method of replacement. Cutting the ropes and replacing them, or undoing the chains temporarily, would make it possible to open the door and put the plate back in position, if no other method could be used. The malleable plate was evidently regarded as inferior, since it might show signs of the work done on it.

THE RACK TEST

Old-time torture methods were of great interest to Houdini. They are mentioned in various notes, and it appears to have been his intention to adapt some of these ancient devices to produce sensational escapes. Most of his notes on this subject are incomplete or are given merely as suitable ideas to be studied later on; for escapes of this type were not offered as challenges, since the apparatus was of obsolete design. Houdini studied every object that could possibly be used to hold him, and was constantly creating new ideas for making escapes; where instruments of torture were concerned, research was necessary. The rack escape was worked out in detail. Houdini planned to construct a rack that would closely resemble the torture device of mediaeval times; and he found an ingenious way in which it could be made into a spectacular escape.

Let us consider the rack as it would appear on the stage. The performer is placed on a bench, and his feet are secured at the lower end. There is a roller at the upper end, and his hands are attached there by other ropes. Then the roller is turned with a crank, until the performer is stretched to the limit, as prisoners were once prepared for torture. The handle of the roller is clamped to the floor or is held by members of the committee, through an opening in the curtain. The performer is in a position where he cannot gain slack by any of the methods generally used. The test is therefore an extraordinary rope tie.

Houdini's diagrams show one roller at the head of the rack; from his notes it appears that two rollers would be preferable, one at each end of the rack, so that the ropes could be wound from both ends; hence release of the feet would be more difficult than release of the hands. The indication of only one roller in the diagrams is explained by the fact that the secret lies in the hand roller alone. The use of two rollers has a certain advantage. The rack is of such simple construction that no preparation seems possible, and the device will stand examination by the most careful committee. But it is a fact that slack is required to escape from ropes, and the rack is designed to prevent slack. Therefore to make the escape sure and effective, a hidden mechanism is highly important.

The preparation planned by Houdini concerned the top roller, which passed through two wooden braces or holes in the frame of the rack. These were necessary to keep the roller in positon. The roller was to be separated at both points where it passed through the frame; that is, the roller consisted of three sections, a long one between two short ones. To keep the roller intact, Houdini designed square-shaped plugs fitting in holes in the sections of the rollers. The handles on each side of the roller kept the end portions from coming out. The divisions between the sections were small, but by pulling the plugs outward, they would slide back in slots and release the center section, which could not, however, come free of the braces. The ends of these plugs were attached to cords running down through the supporting legs of the frame. Both were attached to a single cord and so arranged that a pull would draw back the plugs and release the center section of the roller. The cord ran off-stage or to a place where an assistant could pull it without being observed. As soon as the curtains were closed, the pull was to be given, and the center part of the roller would revolve backward when drawn by the performer, giving him plenty of slack and making it an easy matter for him to release his hands from the roller. A removable section would simplify the process, but it would be more difficult to conceal as perfectly; hence it was not so desirable as the non-removable section. Intricate knots were not the factor that prevented escape; the tension of the rollers was responsible; hence the reverse rolling of the center section was considered sufficient.

In winding the roller as one piece, a complication would present itself; namely, the turning of the release cord with the roller. This shows the advantage of the roller for the feet, and indicates a method of procedure that was not stated, but that appears quite obvious.

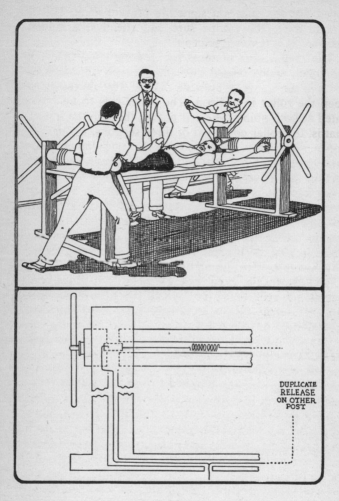

DUPLICATE
RELEASE
ON OTHER
POST

APPEARANCE AND CONSTRUCTION OF THE RACK ESCAPE

First the performer's feet and hands should be bound very tightly, and slack taken up by turning the foot roller. When the hand roller is reached, all slack is gone, and it cannot be turned far without hurting the performer, which is not the purpose for which this rack is intended. The hand roller is not turned far enough to interfere with the pull of the cord releasing the center section of the roller.

Once free from the rack, the performer was able to turn the roller back to its original position, the ropes being slack. To insert the square connecting plugs, a thin pin could be used to push them back into position; but the better plan is to have them return automatically, actuated by springs in the roller either at the ends or by a long thin spring running entirely through the center section and connecting with both plugs. With this mechanical device, the assistant merely draws back the release cord and fastens it so that the plugs are out of the way and the performer can begin his escape immediately. Off the rack, the performer cuts or unhooks the release cord from within the cabinet, and the plugs go back into position.

Houdini typed the description of this trick in Bremen, Germany. The date is not given. A magazine article (date also unknown) which described various forms of torture devices was attached to the material written by Houdini.

THE SPANISH MAIDEN ESCAPE

The escape from the Spanish Maiden was evidently part of Houdini's scheme to produce some day a scene in which the stage would be filled with strange relics of ancient inquisitions, from any one of which he could effect an escape! The rack and the Spanish Maiden are the only two that are explained in his notes, but there are references to others. The Spanish Maiden is a modi-

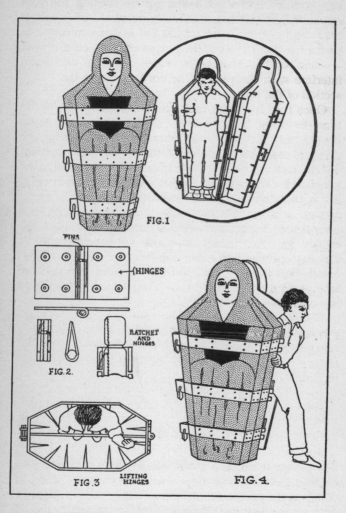

FIG. 1

PINS

HINGES

RATCHET
AND
HINGES

FIG. 2.

FIG. 3   LIFTING
HINGES

FIG. 4.

THE ESCAPE FROM THE SPANISH MAIDEN

fication of the famous instrument of torture. It is a box that stands upright, with a hinged section that opens outward. It is shaped roughly like the human body, and the front is painted to resemble a maiden. Both parts of the box are alike—the box proper and the cover—and the interior of each section is lined with spikes. In this detail it differs from the ancient Iron Maiden, for whereas the spikes were arranged so as to pierce the person imprisoned within, those of the modernized device merely surround the prisoner so that it is impossible for him to move freely. When the Maiden is closed, padlocks may be attached to staples in order to make escape apparently impossible. There are three padlocks; the iron bands to which they are attached pass around the Spanish Maiden and terminate in the hinges.

The secret of the escape from the Spanish Maiden lies in hinges that are specially made. They are pin hinges, but each pin is cut like a ratchet on one side, and two springs inside the tube hold the pin in position. When the box is open, the pins cannot be removed from the hinges. This is because the lower spring swings around with the hinge and engages a groove in the opposite side of the pin. Any attempt to pull the pin upward will fail. When the Spanish Maiden is closed, both springs engage the ratchet; the upper spring is designed to raise the pin from the hinge, the lower spring to keep the pin from falling.

By gripping one of the spikes at the hinge side of the cover (or front section of the box) the performer can lift the cover upward a fraction of an inch. The looseness of the padlocks permits this. Each time he lifts up and releases, the upper spring of each hinge works on the ratchet in the pin, and thus the pins are gradually forced out of the springs.

When the operation has been completed, the pins are clear of the hinges and the performer opens the box at that side, the padlocks serving as hinges. After the escape, the performer replaces the pins by pushing them up through the hinges from the bottom. Everything is secure once more, and the spiked box may be inspected by the committee. When the box is closed, no one will detect the ingenious method of removing the pins from the hinges; when it is opened, the pins cannot be removed. Hence the mode of escape is indetectable, for it is only workable by the person who is confined inside.

CONCLUSION

In summarizing Houdini's escapes, one is impressed by the great number and variety of ideas employed by this famous performer. There seems to have been no limit to the extent of his research and experiment; yet it is safe to say that the material contained in Houdini's notes represents but a fraction of the amazing knowledge that he possessed on this subject. In the literature on magic and conjuring there has been very little reference to escape work, and the known methods have been few and restricted. It is an unquestioned fact that Houdini stands alone as the great creative genius of escapes. There have been other performers who have possessed originality and ingenuity in this field of mystery, but it is probable that the ideas and methods created or planned by Houdini have far exceeded the combined total of all those devised by others. The tendency of escape artists has been to feature one successful escape as long as possible, whereas Houdini was always seeking the new and seemingly impossible; and this collection of Houdini's secrets bears testimony to that fact.

Just as these notes represent a portion of Houdini's total knowledge of the subject, so his escape work represented a portion of his studies and endeavors in the field of mystery. As a magician, Houdini was always seeking the new and the spectacular, always seeking to create some new trick or illusion. As an investigator of fraudulent psychic phenomena he was constantly alert, and he learned many tricks of mediums that other magicians had failed to detect. His unpublished notes on these subjects contain many of the unusual features found in his escape secrets. For in all branches of magic Houdini was a constant seeker of knowledge and a man of originality in ideas and methods.